2nd Workshop on Semantic Representation of Spoken Language 2009

(SRSL 2009)

Held in conjunction with EACL 2009

Athens, Greece
30 March 2009

ISBN: 978-1-61738-557-5

Printed from e-media with permission by:

Curran Associates, Inc.
57 Morehouse Lane
Red Hook, NY 12571

Some format issues inherent in the e-media version may also appear in this print version.

Printed by Curran Associates, Inc. (2010)

For permission requests, please contact the Association for Computational Linguistics at the address below.

Association for Computational Linguistics
209 N. Eighth Street
Stroudsburg, Pennsylvania 18360

Phone: 1-570-476-8006
Fax: 1-570-476-0860

acl@aclweb.org

Additional copies of this publication are available from:

Curran Associates, Inc.
57 Morehouse Lane
Red Hook, NY 12571 USA
Phone: 845-758-0400
Fax: 845-758-2634
Email: curran@proceedings.com
Web: www.proceedings.com

Preface

We are delighted to present you with this volume containing the papers accepted for presentation at the SRSL 2009, the 2nd Workshop on Semantic Representation of Spoken Language, held in Athens, Greece, on March 30th 2009.

The aim of the SRSL 2009 workshop is to bring together researchers interested in the semantic representation of spoken corpora, especially spontaneous speech. On one hand, the semantic gap between contents conveyed by natural languages and their formal representations is a burning aspect in tasks such as information extraction and corpus annotation. The current state-of-the-art supports solutions from very different backgrounds and perspectives, but still remain important and complex issues to deal with, such as the accurate segmentation of speech in semantic units. The discussion of those aspects are one of the main reasons for this workshop. On the other hand, spoken language is a pending issue in computational linguistics and artificial intelligence, both traditionally focused on written language, although semantic processing of speech is necessary for the understanding of both natural and human-machine interaction. Finally, the problems found when trying to linguistically structure spontaneous speech are leading to works focused on its semantic representation. In-depth research on the semantic representation of speech can provide us with a suitable basis for further analysis of related linguistic levels, like prosody or pragmatics.

This event is a highly collaborative effort and we are grateful to all those who helped us construct the program: the authors for submitting their research results; the reviewers for delivering their reviews and discussing them whenever there was some disagreement; and the EACL 2009 organizers for their support.

Wishing you a very enjoyable time at SRSL 2009!

Manuel Alcántara-Plá and Thierry Declerck
SRSL 2009 Program Chairs

SRSL 2009 Organizers

General Chairs:

Manuel Alcántara-Plá, Universidad Autónoma de Madrid (Spain)
Thierry Declerck, DFKI GmbH, Language Technology Lab, Saarbruecken (Germany)

SRSL 2009 Program Committee

Program Chairs:

Manuel Alcántara-Plá, Universidad Autónoma de Madrid (Spain)
Thierry Declerck, DFKI GmbH, Language Technology Lab, Saarbruecken (Germany)

Program Committee Members:

Christina Alexandris, National University of Athens (Greece)
Enrique Alfonseca, Google Zurich (Switzerland)
Paul Buitelaar, DFKI GmbH (Germany)
Harry Bunt, Universiteit van Tilburg (The Netherlands)
Nicoletta Calzolari, ILC-CNR (Italy)
Raquel Fernández Rovira, ILLC-University of Amsterdam (The Netherlands)
Anette Frank, Universität Heidelberg (Germany)
Johannes Matiasek, OFAI (Austria)
Massimo Moneglia, Università degli Studi di Firenze (Italy)
Juan Carlos Moreno Cabrera, Universidad Autónoma de Madrid (Spain)
Antonio Moreno Sandoval, Universidad Autónoma de Madrid (Spain)
Gael Richard, École Nationale Supérieure des Télécommunications, GET-ENST (France)
Carlos Subirats, Universitat Autònoma de Barcelona (Spain)
Isabel Trancoso, Universidade Técnica de Lisboa (Portugal)

Table of Contents

Extreme case formulations in Cypriot Greek

Maria Christodoulidou
Frederick Institute of Technology
7, Y. Frederickou St., Palouriotisa, Nicosia 1036 Cyprus
pre.mc@fit.ac.cy

Abstract

This article is concerned with Extreme Case Formulations (ECFs) (Edwards, 2000; Pomerantz, 1986) in spontaneous Cypriot Greek conversations.[1] This study confirms the occurrence of ECFs in complaints as identified by Edwards (2000) Pomerantz (1986), but goes one step further to analyse the sequential and interaction work accomplished with ECFs in reporting "opposition-type stories" (Schegloff, 1984) and in complaining about a non-present party's misbehaviour. Opposition-type stories report the oppositional conversation of the teller with a third non-present party (id.). Interestingly, in the conversational extracts examined in this study, the conversation reported is culminated with the opponent's reported extreme claim (ECF) occupying the last turn. The occurrence of an ECF at that marked place, that is, at the punchline of the telling, is associated with issues of affiliation and stance since it is placed exactly before the recipient's slot upon story completion, which is a regular place for the occurrence of evaluation (Schegloff, 1984).

1 Introduction

This article reports some of the findings of a study of *extreme case formulations* (ECFs) (Edwards, 2000; Pomerantz, 1986) in spontaneous conversations exclusively conducted in Cypriot Greek.

In a seminal article, Pomerantz (1986) drew attention to the conversational uses of *extreme case formulations* (ECFs). Edwards (2000: 347-8) explains that ECFs are "descriptions or assessments that deploy extreme expressions such as every, all, none, best, least, as good as it gets, always, perfectly, brand new, and absolutely". Pomerantz (1986: 219-220) summarizes the three main uses of ECFs, mainly used in complaints, in the following way:

(1) to assert the strongest case in anticipation of non-sympathetic hearings,
(2) to propose the cause of a phenomenon,
(3) to speak for the rightness (wrongness) of a practice.

Pomerantz's (1986) three uses of ECFs are basically oppositional and argumentative, occurring in environments where descriptions and assessments are being strengthened or resisted. As Edwards (2000) showed this applies to his counselling data (1995) too, where wife and husband produce and defend opposed versions of facts. In this data a lot of ECFs follow the same sequential pattern of "ECF-challenge-softener". Although Pomerantz (1986) did not pursue post-ECF talk, she noted the challenge after an ECF.

However, as Edwards notes (2000: 360), ECFs can also occur in affiliative sequences as "upgrades and displays of affiliation being done, of agreement being full and so on" –as in Pomerantz's (1984) demonstration of how

[1] Cyprus is an independent island republic in the Eastern Mediterranean. Data from the 2001 census of population showed that on 1st October 2001 the total population of the Cyprus Republic was 689,565 composed of 89.7% Greek Cypriots, 0.2% Armenian, 0.5% Maronites, 0.04% Cypriots of European origin called "Latins" and 0.05% Turkish Cypriots; 0.1% did not declare their ethnic religious group (Census of Population 2001); the remainder being foreigners from Europe and Asia. The Greek speech community in Cyprus is defined as diglossic. Diglossia in Cyprus refers to the simultaneous use of the dialect (Cypriot Greek dialect, CD) and the demotic Greek (Modern Greek, MG).

Proceedings of EACL 2009 Workshop on Semantic Representation of Spoken Language - SRSL 2009, pages 1–9,
Athens, Greece, 30 March 2009. ©2009 Association for Computational Linguistics

upgraded "second assessments" display agreement. ECFs make excellent upgrades (id.). Added to this role, ECFs might be treated by participants as "indexing the speaker's stance or attitude", what Edwards calls "investments" (op.cit.: 363-4). As Edwards explains (id.) denying or insisting on something in an extreme way can highlight the action of denying or insisting, as a kind of stance or attitude (cf. Edwards & Potter, 1992; Potter 1996). Finally, Edwards (2000: 365) draws attention to the "nonliteral or metaphoric uses of ECFs" used in actions of exaggerating, teasing, ironizing, emphasizing, joking etc.

2 Data and Methodology

The study of ECFs investigated in this work is based on recordings of informal, spontaneous, face-to-face conversations among close friends or relatives. These are exclusively conducted in Cypriot Greek. The conversations transcribed for the present study are part of a collection of recordings that took place between December 1998 and April 2003. They comprise transcriptions of 35 hours of tape-recorded natural interactions produced by young native Cypriot Greek speakers during a variety of gatherings or occasions, e.g. dinner, gathering for coffee in friends' houses etc. The extracts included in this article comprise transcriptions of approximately 3 hour. The recordings consist of same sex conversations among women.[2]

The method that is adopted in the analysis of the data is Conversation Analysis (CA), which has its origins in the pioneering work in the sixties by the sociologist Harvey Sacks (1992a, 1992b).

First and foremost, conversation analysis has focused its analytical attention on "recorded, naturally occurring talk-in-interaction" (Hutchby and Wooffitt, 1998: 14). These recordings of actual speech are transcribed using a system which is intended to capture in detail the characteristics "of the sequencing of turns, including gaps, pauses and overlaps; and the element of speech delivery such as audible breath and laughter, stress, enunciation, intonation and pitch" (Hutchby and Drew, 1995: 182).

The transcription symbols used in this study are based on the transcription conventions developed by Jefferson for the analysis of conversational turns in English conversation (see Sacks, Schegloff and Jefferson, 1974) and are adopted in the form presented by Ochs, Schegloff and Thompson (1996) and Clift (1999). The relevant transcription symbols for this study are cited in appendix I.

The phonetic inventory used for reading transcription is based on the International Phonetic Association [IPA] which is adjusted to the Greek language by Nespor (1999) and on the phonetic inventory of Cypriot Greek presented and described by Newton (1972).

3 ECFs in Cypriot Greek

My data of spontaneous Cypriot-Greek conversations confirms Edwards's (2000) and Pomerantz's claim (1986) of the use of ECFs in making complaints.

In particular, this study reports a pattern of the sequential and interactional position of ECFs found in the reporting of "opposition-type stories" (Schegloff, 1984) and in complaining about a non-present party's misbehaviour. In the conversations examined here, complaining is expressed with the narration of two-party opposition-type stories in which the teller is one of the two parties involved. In particular, opposition-type stories are reported using the BCBC format, B being the teller and C his/her opponent. Thus, that BCBC format tracks not only the alternation of the turns but also the alternation of positions. This formula turns out to have C's position be the one occupying the last turn (Schegloff, 1984). By "reproducing the "original" utterance or utterances, speakers can provide access to the interaction being discussed, enabling the recipient to assess it for himself. Supplying this kind of evidence is important when…..a complaint is made about someone based on what they said" (Holt, 1996: 229).

It seems that the basic feature attributed to opposition type stories is that they are more than any other form of storytelling "recipient

[2] ECFs were also identified in a set of data collected during 2007 in conversations among young men. The transcription revealed use of ECFs as upgraded assessments and in actions of joking and exaggerating. Interestingly, no use of ECF in complaints was found.

designed" (Sacks, 1971: 453). If this is so, it means that tellers design the storytelling with an orientation to the specific recipients in order to elicit their affiliative siding. In the fragments under study where the teller is one of the opposing parties, it is obviously important for the teller to transmit to her recipients the correctness or appropriateness of her position and the incorrectness or inappropriateness of her opponent's position. In these extracts the teller invests special effort in constructing the contrast between herself and her opponent in two interrelated ways. Therefore, this is accomplished by narrating an opposition-type story based on the conversation she had with the opponent and by reporting the activities of the opponent parties which proposes the significance of the upcoming reported speech. Each story culminates in a report of the other's speech. The motivation for the reporting of speech and activities is grounded in considerations of affiliation and stance.

Actually in the conversations examined in this paper the oppositional story has its punchline in the reporting of an ECF attributed to the third non-present party. One thing the recipient can do is to side with one or the other, that is, teller/protagonist or his/her opponent. Usually recipients side with tellers because this is how tellers choose their story recipients (Schegloff, 1984). In the cases here the reported ECF is responded to with a challenge taking the form of rhetorical question, extreme case formulation, idiomatic expression or ironic evaluation. Stories involve extended single turns at talk (Sacks, 1968: 18). The storytelling sequence is composed "of three serially ordered and adjacently placed types of sequences": "the preface, the telling, and the response sequences" (Sacks, 1974: My main interest is in the punchline and the recipient's slot upon story completion.

Due to the limit of space, I present only two representative examples of the use ECF in the punchline of opposition-type stories as shown in the extract 1 and 2 that follow.

(1)

(D = Dorina; T = Themis; M = Maria; C = Christiana; L = Litsa; N = Nitsa. All of the women participating in the conversation except Dorina are teachers working in the same school. Dorina is a psychologist qualified by the Ministry of Education to visit some specific primary schools and check the welfare of children. Now she is narrating the story of a child in one of the schools she visited.)

1. D emenan ipem mu enam moron, ioθetas
2. me? pu kseri to moro ti leksi tuti::?
3. T indam ↑bu jine?
4. D ioθetas me? lei mu, iδe stom Mama
5. kati ioθesies ce lipa::,
6. T ioθetas me? ipe su?
7. D ioθetas me? lali mu.
8. M ma pco moro?
9. D ena:: pu to eδernen i mamma tu δame::
10. ospu tʃ' espurtisen do:: δerma::n.
11.C ciri' eleison.
12.D eδernen do me ti guta::lan sto iδio
13. simio,
14.C ↑a::!
15.D me ti gutalan ti ksilini sto iδio simio
16. ospu tʃ ↑eskasen do δerman.
17.C ciri' eleison.
18.L ja onoma tu θeu δilaδi (.) jenika etsi
19. aspu-=
20.D =tilefono ti::s tʃe leo tis, cita:: [etsi,
21.C [na su po
22. kati? eγo δen anteχa etsi me etsi
23. aθropus tʃe tora eχasa tin psiχremiam
24. mu [(nomizo).
25.D [to moron effuskomeno δame, leo
26. tis, θa se kataɲɟilo stin astinomia::,
27. frontise mesa se mɲan evδomaδa na
28. jinis mana::, aʎos θa se kataɲɟilo stin
29. astinomia::, poso χrono, ise si? lei mu.
30. erotise me tʃe poson χronon im' eγ(h)o,
31. ise mana? lei mu.
32.→ MO::non Otan θa ji::nis mana θa
33. katalavis lei mu.
34.C a nne::? pe ti::ç.
35.T δe re efcice tʃe pupan::no.
36.L i manes eδδernun ta mora tus me tes
37. kutales.
38.N an ine na jino san esena pe tis
39. kalittera::,

Translation

1. D a child told me, won't you adopt me?
2. how does a child know this wo::rd?
3. T ↑what happened?
4. D won't you adopt me? he told me, he

5. saw something of Mama's[3] show about adoptions and stu::ff,
6. T he told you won't you adopt me?
7. D won't you adopt me? he says to me.
8. M what child?
9. D one:: that was being beaten by his
10. mother, here::, till the:: ski::n cracked.
11.C Jesus Christ.
12.D she hit him with a spoo::n on the same
13. spot,
14.C ↑o::!
15.D with a wooden spoon on the same spot
16. till the skin cr↑acked.
17.C God have mercy.
18.L for God's sake, really (.) just like
19. th-=
20.D =I called he::r up and said loo::k,[right,
21.C [let
22. me tell you something, I couldn't stand
23. this sort of people, I am even losing my
24. temper [now.
25.D [the child is swollen here, I tell
26. her, I'll report you to the poli::ce. I
27. give you one week and you make sure
28. you be a mothe::r to him, otherwise I'll
29. report you to the police, how old, she
30. says to me, are you? she asked me how
31. old I(h) was, are you a mother? she
32. → says. O::nly WHEn you become a
33. mother will you understand she says.
34.C oh rea::lly? you should tell he::r.
35.T she's got a nerve to talk.
36.L mothers don't beat their children with
37. wooden spoons.
38.N if I am to become like you, tell her,
39. then I'd bette::r,

In extract 1 above the complaining proceeds as follows: the teller is reporting the complainable behavior of her opponent through reporting her transgressions (1: 9-10, 12-13, 15-16) and then continues with the reporting of the oppositional exchange (1: 20, 25-33) between her and her opponent which follows the BCBC format. The oppositional exchange culminates in a piece of formulaic-sounding wisdom proffered by the mother (1: 32-33: "only when you become a mother will you understand") which is hearable as an "extra-ordinary" claim (Pomerantz, 1986) framed as such based on the use of the ECF "only" followed with the idiomatic expression "when you become a mother will you understand". According to Torode, "an extreme case is designed to close an argument. As such it is vulnerable to attempts at refutation" (1996: 10). Thus, the placement of that extraordinary claim at the climax of the story should be seen in relation to motivations of eliciting affiliation. In other words the teller offers to the recipient an extreme claim in order to elicit a refutation of that claim. The reporting of the opponent's words effected by intonation, as it is shown in the stress in voice and the louder tone, serves to detach the teller from commitment with these words. In 1: 34 the recipient challenges the mother's exaggerative claim with a rhetorical question "oh rea::lly?". In agreement with Schegloff's claim, the suggested response gets heard as a slot in the oppositional conversation reported by the teller because it comes off "as a proposed piece" of the teller's argument (1984: 46-47). The shift of footing (Goffman, 1979) from the mother's reported extreme claim to the rhetorical question frames (Goffman, 1974) the evaluation as irony.

The following extract also serves to illustrate the point shown with extract 1 about the occurrence of ECF at the climax of an oppositional story.

(2)

(C = Christiana; M = Maria; A = Angelina; P = Petra. Lina is a non-present pary whom the participants usually criticize. Lina, Christiana, and Panos (C's ex-boyfriend) were in the same class as BA students. The following year Lina and Panos continued with masters' degrees. Panos found a job. Lina has just finished her master's and she is very proud of it. This annoys the girls very much. Now she is looking for a job.)

1. C Aku:: tʃ' i LIna-- tʃe proχtes pu milusame
2. [ja ta epaɲɟelmata:: ti mu lali emena::?
3. P [ma ti allo ( )
4. C e eγo, lei mu, an epcanna kamɲan
5. eftakoʃan pu p- mallon enna pcanni o
6. Panos lei mu::, mpts lei mu::
7. M bravo.
8. C enna mini tʃame pu ine? leo tis re, a
9. δδen ton efχaristi:: tʃe vri kati allon
10. enna fii:: leo ti::s. lei mu:: ma
11. sovaromilas? pcanni toso misθo tʃ'
12. enna fii? [leo tis jati na mini,
13.P [e ma'n dʒ' en da lefta to

[3] Mamas is a Cypriot journalist.

14. pan.
15.C a δδen ton efχaristi i δuʎa pu kamni? =
16.P =ma oi mono ja tʃinon ja ullon toŋ
17. gosmon.
18.C nne a δδen ton efχaristi enna fi::i tʃe
19. laLI:: mu:::: e lei mu emenan ammu
20. eδiusasin eftakoʃes lires tʃe na mu
21.→ lalusan fkalle kko::py Ulli mera, θa ta
22. fkalla::
23. (2)
24.A e >to ma :ster pu eʃi e ja na fka::lli
25.→ kko::pi Ulli me::ra<?
26.M .hhh χm χm χm χm.
27.A ɲoθo polla kurazmeni.

Translation

1. C Liste::n, also Lina-- the other day too
2. that we were talking [about jo::bs, you know what she said to me::?
3. P [what else ( )
4. M exa::ctly.
5. C well, I, she tells me, if I was paid some
6. seven hundred pounds as- which is
7. probably what Panos gets she says to
8. me::, mpts she says will he stay put? I say
9. if it doesn't plea::se him and he finds
10. something else, he will qui::t I said. she
11. says to me are you serious? he gets such
12. a salary and he'll quit? [I say, why should he stay on,
13.P [but money isn't
14. everything.
15.C what if he doesn't like his job?=
16.P =and this is not just for him, it goes for
17. everybody.
18.C yes, if he doesn't like it, he'll quit and
19. she sAY::s to me::, well she says if
20. they gave me seven hundred pounds
21. → and told me make photocopies All
22. da::y, I wou::ld.
23. (2)
24.A well >what did she get a ma::ster's for,
25. → to ma::ke co::pies All day::?<
26.M hm hm hm hm
27.A I feel so tired.

In extract (2) the teller announces that the complaint is about something the other (Lina) said to her (2: 1-2) and starts reporting the other's words (2: 5-7), but restarts by reporting the "opposition" type story from an earlier point (2: 7-12).

This inserted oppositional story is hearable as background information essential for the recipients' appreciation of the punchline. The punchline, that is, the opponent's words that she started reporting in 2: 5-7, but were left unreported, are repeated and completed in 2: 16-18. In this story the teller presents the oppositional conversation in a BCBC format where B is the teller and C the opponent, that is, Lina. The opponent is reported as making the questions and the teller as responding to them. The reported questions are presented as aggressive and challenging of the responses given by the teller (2: 9-10, "are you serious? he gets such a salary and he'll quit?"). With the reported assessment of 2: 19-22, Lina is presented as expressing her overt disapproval of Panos's claims which are also adapted by Christiana. This is achieved with her reported exaggerated claim that even if she was asked to do copying she would do it for the money. This becomes even more extreme because it is accompanied with an "extreme case formulation" ("all day"). This is a strong criticism of the teller and her friend's beliefs. Christiana is complaining about her making such a strong criticism of their beliefs. The mimicked exaggeration in reproducing the opponent's words effected with stretch and emphasis clearly detaches the teller from their inside meaning.

The reported claim is responded to with a rhetorical question by one of the recipients (2: 24-25). This question is hearable as a slot in the oppositional conversation reported by the teller because it comes off as a piece of the complainant's argument. With that she challenges the opponent's claim by bringing it into question. The repetition of the extreme case formulation "all day" is employed to challenge the extreme claim of the opponent. This question is framed as an ironic challenge based on the impossibility of what is being asked "well >what did she get a master's for, to make copies all day?<" reinforced with the "extreme case" "all day?". This question serves as an ironic challenge on another level too, that of the shared knowledge that Lina is very proud of having a master's degree so her claim is not true. Hence, with this question the recipient claims disbelief of the opponent's assessment. In addition, this question serves as an "impossible description" (Torode, 1996).

As was mentioned above ECFs do not only occur in reporting and responding to opposition-type stories, but also in complaining about a non-present party's misbehavior in general. Extract 3 that follows is a representative example of that case.

(3)

(C = Christiana; M = Maria; A = Angelina; P = Petra; E = Eleana. Before the following conversation Christiana was narrating the previous night in the club a young guy was flirting with her, but she was ignoring him. The conversation is about that guy and Andie, a non-present party)

1. C ((to E)) θima::SE::! [to
2. M [hu
3. C sinδromo tis Andi::ς!
4. M ti sinδromon eʃi?
5. C → opcos mas mila pai tʃe pcanni ton tʃe
6. mila ↑tu::!
7. E o::,
8. C pu tʃin din-- en di θimase tʃin din imera
9. pu rt- tʃin da peθca ta:: [i fili tis i
10. Lemeʃani::?
11. A [mem mu to
12. ksanapi::s re Xristiana::.
13.C tiz LIZA::S?
14.E pu tan na mas proksenepsi::
15. telospanton.
16.C ne
17.E tʃinus.
18.C→ tʃ' o::pcos ercetun tʃe milam mas
19. ercetun tʃ' epcanen ton etsi i Andi:: tʃ'
20. epienne tʃ' emilan ↑tu::!
21.E e? (.) ekamen do tʃe pse::s?
22.C epie tʃ' epcan ton tʃin dom mitsi
23. peθca::.
24.M e oi re, °ton aγnosto::°?
25.C nne::.
26.G enna firto::
27.C etravisen don =
28.E =ma tora sovara::?=
29.C = tʃinos itan etsi:: to χore- o χoros tu
30. etsi polla pros to polla proklitiko::s
31. susto::s [ksero 'γo::,
32.A [χm χm χm.
33.C tʃe χorefce [tʃinos
34.E [inda,
35.C tʃ' i Andi [[δame mes ta
36.E [[pco θarros!
37.C poθca tu tʃe χorefkan kolliti etsi::.
38.M ↑ate re::?
39.A ma sovaromila::s?
40.P → tʃ' [u::lli mera vura tom bater pu piso::
41. tʃini::?
42.A [tʃ' i Liza ti tis ipen?
43.C ↑tipoTE::.

Translation

1. C ((to E)) ((do you)) reme::MBE::R!
2. [Andie's syndrome::!
3. [hu
4. M what is her syndrome?
5. C→ every time someone is talking to us
6. she starts talking to hi::m?
7. E n::,
8. C since th-- don't you remember that
9. day that those guys [LIZA's friends
10. from Limassol?
11.A [don't say that
12. agai::n re Christiana::.
13.C came?
14.E that she was going to introduce to us
15. actually.
16.C yes.
17.E those.
18.C→ and e::very time someone was
19. talking to us Andie was coming and
20. pulling him one side like that and
was talking to ↑hi::m!
21.E so? (.) did she do that last ni::ght
too?
22.C she went and pulled that young guy
23. to one side, guy::s.
24.M oh no re, °the strange::r°?
25.C ye::s.
26.G I'll faint.
27.C she pulled him closer=
28.E =now seriously::?=
29.C =he was so::rt the d- his dancing was
30. sort of very provocative shaking
31. [for example::,
32.A [hm, hm, hm
33.C and he was [dancing
34.E [what,
35.C and Andie [[here within his,
36.E [[a nerve!
37.C legs and they were dancing stuck like
glue like tha::t.
38.M ↑oh really re::!
39.A seriously::?
40.P → so [does she spend a::ll her time with
41. the priest?
42.A [and what did Liza say to her?
43.C ↑nothI::Ng.

As was mentioned above in complaints it is important for the teller to establish his/her recipients' affiliation. In my data, where the teller is complaining about another, this is usually achieved with extreme and hyperbolic descriptions of the other's misbehaviour.

Thus, in 3: 1-3 the teller introduces a complaint about a non-present party's misbehaviour by soliciting a "reminiscence recognition" from E, the knowing recipient (cf. Lerner, 1992: 255) about the principal character's (cf. Goodwin, 1984) behaviour. By characterizing Andie's behaviour as a "syndrome", the teller (3: 3) foreshows a negative telling/criticism of Andie and establishes her stance towards the upcoming telling. In addition, through the reminiscence recognition solicit she invites the knowing recipient to confirm what it assesses and express a similar stance. Since the addressed recipient withholds a response, the teller through an extreme description (3: 5-6) identified as such by the ECF "every time" employs a second solicit of reminiscence recognition (3: 5) addressed to E, the knowing recipient. E (3: 6) responds negatively to the solicit and this is in disagreement with the expectations of the solicit. The teller initiates a third solicit of reminiscence recognition (3: 8-10) and finally receives recognition by the knowing recipient (3: 14-15). The ECF "every time" is repeated by the teller (3:18-20) in a last attempt to receive recognition. The addressed recipient with a "candidate understanding" (Wilkinson and Kitzinger, 2006) in the form of a question (3: 21) reveals recognition of the connection between the information given in the preface and the topic of the upcoming telling, that is, what the story is about and asks about it directly, "so? (.) did she do that last ni::ght too?".

The telling (3: 22-23) is designed as a surprise source as shown by the fact that it responds to a yes/no question (3: 21) with a detailed description of the third person's misconduct and the placement of the address form "guy::s" in turn final position. The telling is responded to by the recipient (3: 24) with an assertion of "ritualized disbelief" (Heritage, 1984: 339) which treats the prior utterance as news (Wilkinson and Kitzinger, 2006). The teller in each of her turns (22-23, 27, 29-31, 33, 35, 37) adds another increment which forms part of the exaggerated description of the transgression of the principal character's behaviour. The description of the other's transgression has its climax in 3: 37.

The recipients, that is, M (3: 38), A (3: 39) and P (3: 40-41) make an evaluation upon the story-completion one after the other. Thus M (3: 38) and A (3: 39) both display "assertions of ritualized disbelief". [4] P (3: 40-41), produces a rhetorical question, identified as such because it does not expect a response since it brings into question a common knowledge. It is framed as ironic evaluation, based on the fact that is not sequentially linked to the previous talk. In addition, the extreme ECF "all her time" adds to the ironic hearing. The ironic evaluation conveyed is also recognized based on the shared knowledge that Andie is visiting a priest often and consults with him. Hence, with this assertion P (3: 40-41) offers another argument for Andie's behaviour being reprehensible by ironically evaluating her incompatible actions. Her behaviour as described by the teller contradicts the fact that she is known to spend a great deal of time with the priest.

4 Conclusion

In this paper I investigated one aspect of the interactional and sequential work accomplished with ECFs in complaining through a description of a non-present party's misbehavior and in reporting opposition-type stories. Specifically, the focus was on complaints about the behaviour of a third non-present party which develops with the reporting of two-party "opposition type" exchanges in which the teller is one of the two parties involved (Schegloff, 1984). The contrasting positions are presented with the BCBC formula with the opponent's position occupying the last turn.

In exploring the sequential positioning of ECFs, I discovered that a regular place of their

[4] These items "treat a prior utterance as news for recipient" (Heritage, 1984: 339), but according to Wilkinson and Kitzinger these kinds of assertions "do more than this: they convey the speaker's amazed incredulity and may also thus constitute a kind of surprise response in their own right" (2006: 34).

occurrence in storytelling sequences is on the punchline of the story and more specifically on the culmination of the reporting of "opposition type" conversation.

The occurrence of ECFs at the end of the telling sequence seems to be associated with issues of affiliation that are sought from the recipients since the "the story recipient's slot after story completion" is a marked place for the occurrence of evaluations where the recipient is expected to side either with the teller or her opponent. (Schegloff, 1984: 44). Thus at this place the teller offers to the recipient something extreme to evaluate and challenge.

In the extracts above recipients respond with evaluations expressed with rhetorical questions which consist of repetitions of "extreme case formulation(s)" (Pomerantz, 1986) and "impossible description(s)" (Torode, 1996) of a third person's overbuilt claim or words.

To sum up extracts (1 & 2) examined in this paper revealed the following pattern:

1. Opposition-type stories BCBC
2. Punchline: Reporting C's ECF
3. Recipient's slot: Challenging the ECF {by non-literal means: rhetorical questions, ironic evaluations, impossible descriptions, repetitions of C's ECF)

Extract 3 revealed the following pattern

Teller: Description of the other's misbehavior with ECFs.
Recipient: Evaluation with ECF

To conclude with this study proves that the occurrence of ECF at the puncline is used to elicit the affiliation of the recipients, who express agreement/affiliation with the teller by challenging the ECF proffered by her opponent. This proves Sacks's (1972: 341) observation that in some sequences certain activities have regular places of occurrence to such an extent that their absence is noticeable. This observation leads "to a distinction between a "slot" and the "items" which fill it and to proposing that certain activities are accomplished by a combination between some item and some slot" (id.).

Appendix I

Transcription System

[[— Separate left square brackets, one above the other on two successive lines with utterances by different speakers, indicates a point of overlap onset, whether at the start of an utterance or later.

= — Equal signs ordinarily come in pairs – one at the end of a line and another at the start of a next line. If the two lines connected by the equal signs are by the same speaker, then there was a single, continuous utterance with no break or pause, which was broken up in order to by different speakers, then the second followed the first

(2) — Numbers in parenthesis indicate silence.

(.) — A dot in parentheses indicates a micropause.

. — The period indicates a falling or final, intonation contour, not necessarily the end of a sentence.

? — A question mark indicates rising intonation, not necessarily a question.

, — A comma indicates continuing intonation, not necessarily a clause boundary.

:: — Colons are used to indicate the prolongation or stretching of the sound just preceding them. The more colons the longer the stretching.

- — A hyphen after a word or part of a word indicates a cut-off or self-interruption, often done with a glottal or dental stop.

word — Underlining is used to indicate stress or emphasis.

WOrd — Capital letters indicate louder than the rest talk.

↑ — The up arrow indicate a segment starting on sharper rise.

> < — The combination of "more than" and "less than" symbols indicates that the talk between them is compressed or rushed.

.hhh — The dot followed by "h's" indicates inbreath

(h) — The letter "h" in parentheses inside the boundaries of a word indicates laughter.

(word) — When all or a part of an utterance is in parentheses, this indicates uncertainty on the transcriber's part, but represents a likely possibility.

( ) — Empty parentheses indicate that something is being said, but no hearing can be achieved.

→ — An arrow marks significant turns.

References

Census of Population 2001 (2003). General demographic characteristics, vol. 1.Statistical Service/Republic of Cyprus.

Clift, R. (1999). Irony in conversation. *Language in Society 28*, 523-553.

Edwards, D. (2000). Extreme case formulations: Softeners, investment, and doing nonliteral. In *Research on Language and Social Interaction 33, 4*, 347-373.

Edwards, D. and Potter, J. (1992). *Discursive psychology*. London: Sage.

Goffman, Erving (1974). *Frame analysis: An essay on the organization of experience.* New York: Harper and Row.

Goffman, Erving (1979). Footing. In Semiotica 25, 1- 29. Reprinted in E. Goffman and D. Hymes (1981) (eds.), *Forms of talk,* 124-161.Philadelphia: University of Pennsylvania Press.

Goodwin, Ch. (1984). Notes on story structure and the organization of participation. In J. M. Atkinson and J. Heritage (eds.), *Structures of social action: Studies in conversation analysis*, 225-246. Cambridge: CUP.

Heritage, J. (1984). *Garfinkel and ethnomethodology*. Cambridge: Polity Press.

Holt, E. (1996). Reporting on talk: the use of direct reported speech inconversation. *Research on Language and Social Interaction 29, 3*, 219-245.

Hutchby, I. and P. Drew (1995). Conversation analysis. In J.Verschueren, J.-O. Östman, J. Blommaert and C. Bulacaen (eds.), *Handbook of pragmatics*, 182-189. Amsterdam, Philadelphia: John Benjamins.

Hutchby, I. and R. Wooffitt (1998). *Conversation analysis*. Cambridge: Polity Press.

Lerner, G. (1992). Assisted storytelling: Deploying shared knowledge as a practical matter. *Qualitative Sociology* 15, 3, 247-271.

Nespor, M. (1999). *Fonologia*. Athens. Patakis

Newton, B. (1972). *Cypriot Greek: its phonology and inflections*. The Hauge: Mouton.

Ochs, E., E. Schegloff and S. A. Thomson (1996) (eds.), *Interaction and grammar*. Cambridge: CUP.

Pomerantz, Anita (1984). Agreeing and disagreeing with assessments: some features of preferred/dispreferred turn shapes. In J. M. Atkinson and J.Heritage (eds.), *Structures of social action: Studies in conversation analysis,* 57-101. Cambridge: CUP.

Pomerantz, A. (1986). Extreme case formulations: A way of legitimizing claims. *Human Studies 9*, 219-230.

Potter, J. (1996). *Representing reality: Discourse, rhetoric, and social construction.* London: Sage.

Sacks, H. (1992a). *Lectures on conversation, [1964-1968],* volume I. Edited by G. Jefferson. Oxford: Basil Blackwell.

Sacks, H. (1992b). *Lectures on conversation, [1968-1972],* volume II. Edited by G. Jefferson. Oxford: Basil Blackwell.

Sacks, H., E. Schegloff, G. Jefferson (1974). A simplest systematics for the organization of turn-taking for conversation. *Language* 50, 696-735.

Schegloff, E. A. (1984). On some questions and ambiguities in conversation. In J. M. Atkinson and J. Heritage (eds.), *Structures of social action: Studies in conversation analysis*, 28-52. Cambridge: CUP.

Torode, B. (1996, July). *Humour as impossible* Mexico.*description: humour and horror in calls to a consumer help line*. Paper delivered at 5th International Pragmatics Conference, Mexico City.

Wilkinson, S. and C. Kitzinger (2006) Surprise as an interactional achievement: Reaction tokens in conversation. *Social Psychology Quarterly* 69, 2, 150-182.

On the segmentation of requests in spoken language

Michael Alvarez-Pereyre
Université Paris-Sorbonne – CELTA
Maison de la recherche (D.310)
28 rue Serpente, 75006 Paris, France
maponline@gmail.com

Abstract

This paper presents a theoretical approach to the characterization of requests boundaries and structure in general spoken dialogue. Emphasis is laid on the fracture between the illocutionary act of requesting (for which the term 'request' is kept) and the locutionary elements that carry it out (its 'instantiation'). This approach leads to a representation of requests based on the inclusion of a semantic level under a pragmatic level via a structural level. These distinctions are meant to benefit to the semantic-pragmatic segmentation of dialogue and the study of request strategies.

1 Introduction

This paper focuses on the segmentation of requests in spoken language from a semantic-pragmatic perspective. Taxonomies exist for specific types of requests,[1] and general dialogue-acts taxonomies like DAMSL cover various types of utterances 'influencing the addressee's future action' (Core and Allen, 1997; Stolcke et al., 2000). The aim is not to replace them—the former are finer-grained than what is proposed here, and the latter have the advantage of treating requests in a framework which includes other types of dialogue acts. The purpose of this paper is rather to contribute to a middle-ground, with distinctions general enough to encompass all types of action requests (assuming that a common process of 'requesting' underlies them), yet detailed and structured enough to account for the construction of their meaning. The goal is therefore not to provide a taxonomy *identifying* speech or dialogue acts in 'shallow' discourse structure (Jurafsky et al., 1997), but a structured *explanatory* taxonomy of requesting means.

The scope is 'requests for action' taken in a broad sense, as exemplified by (1-3).[2]

(1) Err / hmm / you know / it would probably be easiest if I just squeezed back there and poked around myself / would that be alright with you? // (BRO_0h32m56s)

(2) Mister Masry? // [–Yeah //] I was wondering can you tell me who I talk to / about maybe getting an advance on my paycheck // Just / for the week-end // (BRO_0h14m33s)

(3) Now you listen // I don't give a damn / which way you go / just don't follow me / you got that? // (FUG_0h18m59s)

'Request' is understood broadly to include the whole spectrum of invitations, entreaties, commands, etc. 'Action' is understood broadly in the sense that the scope includes requests for clarification (e.g. '*Who* said it?'); for attention, as 'Now you listen' in (3) or 'Mr Masry?' in (2); for confirmation, as 'You got that?' in (3); and of course what corresponds to a narrow understanding of the expression 'action requests', namely requests for actions not concerned with dialogue management, as the request to allow the speaker of (1) into the file room of the county water board, the request to direct the speaker of (2) to the right person, or the request not to follow the speaker of (3). The scope excludes 'true' questions (unmarked information

[1] For instance clarification requests or 'CRs' (Corsaro, 1977; Purver, Ginzburg and Healey, 2003; Purver, 2004; Rodríguez and Schlangen, 2004, among others), check-questions (Jurafsky and Martin, 2000, §19.3), etc.

[2] The sequences quoted in this paper are extracted from a corpus of contemporary North-American films. Though film dialogues can by no means be called 'spontaneous' speech, they share enough features with naturally occurring interactions as to help us define the tools to study requests in spoken language. The advantage of working with commercial films is that such material covers the whole gamut of pragmatic interactions and situations—though, admittedly, as represented not 'intercepted' scenes. Sequences are indexed with three block capitals to identify the film quoted (e.g. *Erin Brockovich*, found at [BRO] in the References) and three numbers specifying the hour, minute and second when the sequence begins. The sound track is transcribed as the succession of speech 'increments' separated by pauses, with simple slashes [/] and double slashes [//] to distinguish between 'tentative' and 'final' pauses, following Pike (1945).

Proceedings of EACL 2009 Workshop on Semantic Representation of Spoken Language - SRSL 2009, pages 10–18,
Athens, Greece, 30 March 2009.

requests in which no significant attempt to further influence the addressee is traced).

The main question of this paper is: What definition of a 'request' should we work with, if we are to describe the outer boundaries and the inner complexity of requests in a way that enables modelization and quantification of request strategies?[3]

Section 2 starts from the difficulty of assigning boundaries to spoken language 'requests' in the framework of traditional speech act theory, and stresses key principles for pragmatic research based on spoken corpora. Section 3 proposes a minimal set of distinctions necessary to account for the inner organization of request instantiations. Section 4 assesses the approach.

2 Towards a definition of 'requests'

One aspect of language interactions which tends to be oversimplified is the relationship between a 'request' and its instantiation.[4] True, with 'indirect requests', traditional pragmatics cast light on the gap between the 'illocutionary act' of requesting and the 'locutionary act' (or the 'literal' elements) used to express it. To bridge this gap, it focused on the contextual felicity-conditions of utterances, or on the conversational implicatures, the maxims, the inference rules or the cognitive faculties that enable us to construe their meaning (Austin, 1962; Searle, 1969; Searle, 1979; Grice, 1975; Perrault and Allen, 1980; Lenci, 1994, etc.); but all too often, the very examples given as a starting point to such analyses are far too simple, as the signifier of the request is almost invariably composed of one isolated, syntactically pure segment.[5] Pragmatic analyses of this kind encourage an idealized vision of language interactions, in which a request (and more generally a speech act) coincides perfectly with one stand-alone, clear-cut and atemporal piece of language.

More recent 'cue-based' (Jurafsky and Martin, 2000) probabilistic approaches, on the other hand, give an increasingly accurate surface description of empirical dialogues as successions of normalized 'moves' or 'dialogue acts' (Carletta et al., 1997; Stolcke et al., 2000); but the normalization of sequences as distinct 'utterances' also encourages an atomistic, 'one segment, one act' vision.[6]

Yet, as far as semantic-pragmatic representation is concerned, it is artificial and problematic to imagine that a request corresponds to a 'block' of signifier (§2.1) and to a 'block' of meaning (§2.2).

2.1 'Requests'—from signs to meaning

Spoken corpora show that requests are rarely composed of one clause or one simple clause-complex (though dialogue management requests might tend to correspond to monosegmental clauses or fragments). The majority of requests take the form of several increments of various syntactic, semantic and pragmatic types, often with repetitions of increments, interruptions from the co-interactants (and from the speakers themselves), embedded phases of negotiation, etc. The safest way to approach the problem is therefore to consider that *a priori* every request instantiation is likely to have a *discontinuous signifier* and *extensible boundaries*.

Requesting: a real-time process

Even assigning the beginning and the end of a 'request' in a linear transcription can prove difficult, as shown by some seemingly simple, supposedly straightforward 'imperative' requests:

(4) Put a light in there // Put a light in there //
(FUG_0h32m59s)

(5) Put that gun down // Put that gun down // Now //
(FUG_0h36m40s)

The police officer who utters (4) points successively at two different locations in a tunnel in which he is walking with his staff. It is therefore not a problem to say that the two clauses in this sequence correspond to two different requests. When some time later the police officer corners a fugitive and shouts (5), this 'bijective' analysis does not hold anymore: the officer does not want *two* separate actions of 'putting the gun down'.

To consider the segment 'Put that gun down' as 'a request' would force us to consider the second

[3] This paper deals primarily with the theoretical foundations of methodology and does not tackle the technical implementation of the results.

[4] 'Instantiation' might be preferred to 'formulation', as the former term makes it clearer that the speech elements uttered participate not so much in the communication as in the *performing* of the request (along with other elements not discussed here such as intonation, gesture, social context, etc.).

[5] Stubbs (1983, p. 148) noted that 'it is something of a paradox that speech act theory emphasizes the uses of language, and in fact applies to utterances not sentences, but has depended largely on introspective judgments of isolated sentences'. Geis (1995) pointed out that acts such as requesting or inviting often develop over several interaction turns.

[6] That these 'utterances' may contribute to conversational or dialogue 'games' (Carletta et al., 1997; Levin et al., 1998, for instance) tends, in practice, to reinforce their atomistic character, despite the fundamental remark by Traum and Hinkelman (1992) on the divisibility of 'utterances'.

segment, as well as 'now', as so many 'requests', since each of the three segments, in the situation, is pronounced in order to trigger an action. It is preferable to say that the three increments instantiate *one* same request. The reason is, that all throughout the speech sequence, the police officer has one result in mind only, and the fulfillment of his request at any moment of the sequence would in fact render the subsequent increments useless and even incoherent (which is not the case in (4)).[7]

The situation of a 'surjective' relationship between the speech increments and the acts they perform occurs in cases like (5) because the instantiation of action-requests rarely fits the ideal scenario according to which one 'block' *stimulus* triggers one clear *reaction* (or not), as summarized in the left part of Figure 1. Spoken language being a real-time process, interactants habitually take into consideration the current state of the world, checking whether their expectations have been met (and probably in a scalar not a polar way), and deciding whether more *stimulation* (seen as process) is necessary. In other words, the perlocutionary (the set of effects of the utterance) may influence the locutionary in return, as long as the world differs from what the speakers would like it to be; and as long as the speakers do not recognize the product of their intention in the world, they have to choose between several options: repeat, rephrase, modify the extent of, or abandon their requests. To account for this, one must consider request-instantiation not as an end-product but as a process, not as 'act' but as action in progress. This is summarized in the right part of Figure 1.

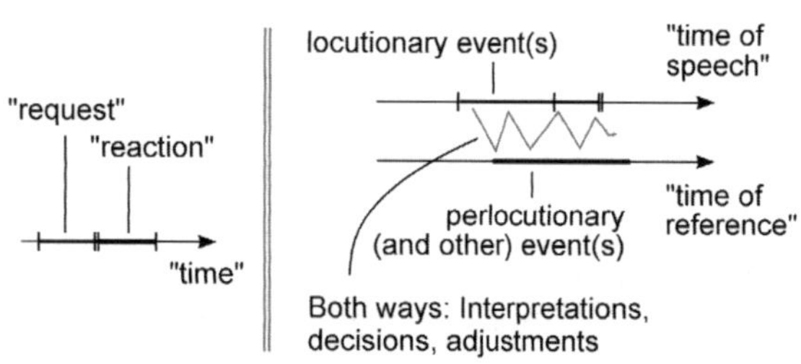

Figure 1: Requesting, a real-time process

[7]Still, it is common for a speaker to add request-related increments of specific types (e.g. stating motives) even after the addressee has started complying. This is because the speaker's goal is usually not just to have the addressee fulfill the request: preserving or attaining a specific kind of relationship with one's interactants (e.g. by sharing one's reasons with them) is an objective in itself, which partly explains the '*variability*' in request strategies (Bloomfield, 1933, §2.6) and sometimes even justifies the withdrawal of a request.

The speech/act fracture

The problem of the instantiation of requests reaches in fact deeper than the 'mere' real-time calculation of an intention/effects (and /cost) ratio on the part of the speaker. Speech being linear, any request that uses spoken language for its instantiation will extend over a certain span. Often, the length of that span is primarily accounted for by the internal *complexity* of the request instantiation, even before it becomes relevant to assess the perlocutionary. That a radical fracture must be acknowledged between the speech elements used and the act performed is exemplified by (6), uttered in an emergency ward by a chief-doctor who is examining a patient, to a fellow doctor who is taking care of another patient a few meters away.

(6) Al / get over here / I need you // (FUG_1h06m42s)

It is tempting to analyze (6) as a request preceded by a specification of its target and followed by an explanation of its motive. The problem with this 'narrow' analysis is that it forces major descriptive changes when possible variants are taken into consideration, such as (6′) and (6″) (assuming that, in the situation, they could have produced the same effect). It seems indeed difficult to describe the increment 'I need you' as a 'request' in (6′) but as a mere explanation, 'banalized' by the presence of the imperative increment, in (6); and it seems equally difficult to hold that the vocative increment 'Al' falls within the scope of the request in (6″) but outside of it in (6).

(6′) Al / I need you //

(6″) Al //

The 'narrow' analysis presented above results from a vision of request instantiations in EITHER/OR terms within a limited range of clear-cut strategies (sometimes reduced to clause-types). However, the comparison of common requests such as (6) with their possible variants shows that the very idea of pinpointing one increment (usually a sentence) as *the* support of the request is taken at fault—so much so that the distinction between 'direct' and 'indirect' speech acts falls. Imperative clauses may retain a specificity compared with other segments (see further on), but the facts remain that (a) countless requests are instantiated by *several* increments, (b) a great number of these increments might suffice to instantiate the corresponding request alone, (c) none of these increments can claim to be '*the* segment of speech that performs the act', and therefore (d) all of the increments, far from excluding one another from the request instantiation, contribute to it.

From this perspective, the semantic-pragmatic segmentation of requests in spoken language consists in, first, identifying the increments involved in 'carrying out' the request and, second, determining the contribution of each increment to the whole. It seems doubtful, however, that the meaning of a request should be the simple, compositional addition of the meanings of its increments. One reason is that the increments of a request are often semantically and pragmatically heterogeneous (the three increments in (6) are by no means equatable), and their modes of contribution are therefore several. If heterogeneity is not a problem for the interactants, it is probably because they rely on a broader and more flexible vision of a request's *meaning* than is often acknowledged.

2.2 Requesting—from intention to signs

Why do speakers formulate requests? In most cases, the goal is not to actually witness an action. The speaker of (4) is not interested in 'seeing' his staff set up spotlights because he said so, nor is the speaker of (6) interested in 'seeing' 'Al' come over to her (if it were the case, motive increments such as 'I need you' would be incoherent, except maybe as ploys). The officer wants the tunnel to be lit, and the doctor wants immediate help from a colleague nearby. Each of these requests is therefore meant to bring about a specific *situation*. To be sure, the ultimate object of most requests is a desired state of the world—not an action; and the possible actions of the co-interactant(s) often have value not of themselves but primarily as a step towards the advent of that state.[8] A useful way to represent the speaker's mental context preceding a request instantiation is therefore to distinguish several 'worlds' roughly seen as static—the current world and the possible worlds (including the target world but also undesired worlds, maybe others still)—separated by a dynamic 'transition situation' which includes the possible actions of the co-interactants and the possibility for the speaker to stimulate them into enacting them.

Stating the reason that makes the target-world desirable ('I need you') or naming, with an imperative, the action that can bring about this world ('Come here'), are two ways, *not mutually exclusive*, to reach the desired situation. Other increments could be added without 'exhausting' the meaning of the request, i.e. without instantiating a new or different one. Thus, the meaning of a request is often alluded to jointly by several elements which emphasize various parameters of the worlds or of the transition situation considered, along with elements referring to the process of requesting itself. Even when a speaker resorts to the imperative in order to call for an action, it is habitually clear to all that this action is to be enacted *in the name of* something else. The functioning of a request is therefore always *metonymic* (i.e. based on a radical speech/act fracture) in the sense that increments focus on one element or another and yet instantiate the whole request.

Requests might therefore be best described not as 'attempts... by the speaker to get the hearer to do something' (Searle, 1979, p. 13) but rather as *attempts to involve the addressee into a plan devised to reach a target world*—a plan defined especially (but never exclusively) by the projected action(s) of the addressee. In this perspective, the increments not naming the projected action are not seen as the conditions meant to help the addressee decode that action (in traditional pragmatic examples, these elements strangely disappear in the presence of the imperative); they are understood here as part of the general strategy of *sharing of a plan* that takes place when a request is instantiated (a 'sharing' which can, of course, be minimal).

3 Towards a 'constituency' of request instantiations

This section details how the reflections developed in §2 can be rendered operational in order to segment request instantiations. The aim here is to sort out the semantic-pragmatic 'constituency' of request instantiations, i.e. the system whereby higher (and often larger) units include lower (often smaller) ones. The task is therefore to find out which ranks are relevant for the study of requests and what primary distinctions should be acknowledged between the units of these ranks.[9]

[8] The idea of 'plan' below is close to that found in Perrault and Allen (1980, §3.3), but its treatment, from the perspective of a linguistic 'geo-strategy', will be different.

[9] The reflection below is presented in a progressive way rather than as a complete nomenclature, both to show the empirical necessity of the distinctions acknowledged, and as a reminder that this model has not reached a definitive phase. Parallels may be found between the Universe, Manners and Phases described below and (respectively) the attentional, linguistic and intentional structures of Grosz and Sidner (1986), though with differences not discussed here.

3.1 Semantic distinctions

Part of what defines a request instantiation is, purely and simply, its 'Universe', understood as *what entities, concepts, qualities and relations are verbalized* (and regardless of the way they are). One level of description (at least) should therefore be dedicated to distinctions between the types of elements that appear in speech. Since the 'Universe' of speakers is not objective but rather peopled and structured by what makes sense in their world-views, some elements are given more prominence than others among the 'worlds' and the 'transition situation' assumed above.

In many request instantiations, the speaker refers to what could be called the '*head-action*' of the request, i.e. the action that should lead most directly to the 'target world': '(Can you) tell me who...' (2), 'Put that gun down' (5), etc. Regularly, however, actions are named which are not the *head-action* of the request. What is verbalized often corresponds either to a '*sub-action*' of the head-action hoped for, or to a '*germane action*' which is not a necessary subpart of the head-action but is, in the context, related to it and meant to trigger it. 'Call' names a *sub-action* in (7), as it is a necessary step within the head-action 'tell'. 'Look at it' names a *germane* action in (8): with this utterance a fisherman asks a shark specialist to reconsider his judgment that the shark under examination (caught by the fisherman) is too small to qualify as the man-eater everyone is hunting for. Though 'Looking' is not properly a sub-action of 'changing one's judgment' (or of 'reconsidering' it), it is supposed, in this context, to lead to that.

(7) ... You call Judge Rubin / you tell him I want a whole bunch of phone-taps... // (FUG_0h29m37s)

(8) What / this is a big mouth / look at it // (JAW_0h33m09s)

Many other verb-referents can be found which are not to be enacted by the addressee, such as 'I was wondering' in (2) or 'You know' in (1). The former is a (mental) process attributed to the first person (P1), the latter is a (mental) state attributed to the second person (P2). An additional difference is that 'I was wondering' is an assertion (of the occurrence of a reflection process) whereas 'You know', in this utterance, hesitates between the question and the assertion (as it often does). This difference relates to a second level of description: actions (and other elements) can be verbalized in different '*manners*', for instance a *directive* or a *descriptive* manner. Following a traditional distinction, the former tells the addressee *to* do the action (through imperatives, performatives and maybe nominals, as in the army's 'Ateeention!') whereas the latter talks *of* or *about* the action (through various types of questions, assertions, exclamations, hypotheses, etc.). In (1), 'It would probably be easiest...' is the (descriptive) assertion of a judgment on '...if I just squeezed back there and poked around myself', in which a sub-action and a higher-action (attributed to the first person, and to be *allowed*, not enacted by the second person) are verbalized as the (descriptive) evocation of a possibility (see Tables 2 and 3).

Other elements than actions are found in the verbalized 'Universe' of a request instantiation. People and objects are often named, some more than others. *Addressees* are crucial interactants as they are often hoped to become the agents of the projected head-actions, and they are therefore often named in separate increments (especially to attract their attention, as in (2), or to modalize the request). In a similar way, the notion of *head-object* can be useful to refer to those objects that occupy a central position in the representation of the head-action. Indeed, head-objects are so important on the 'mind map' of the speaker that they are commonly named without the action itself ('Scalpel' in an operating room, 'The door!', etc.). Sometimes, these objects are accompanied by other elements which help specify what is to be done, especially the *location* where the action is to take place or end. When people, objects, locations or other elements are verbalized outside the net of relationships found in clauses, they are often pointed at through speech, and the manner can be said to be '*indexical*'. Table 1 illustrates the concepts of 'head' action, object and location (FUG_0h36m49s).

(9)	*Hands*	*up*	*Over your head*	*Turn around*
Univ.	h-obj.$_{R1}$	head-location(s)$_{R1}$		h-action$_{R2}$
Manner	idx.	idx.	indexical	directive
	REQUEST 1			REQUEST 2

Table 1: 'Head' actions, objects and locations

If the target-situation is desired (and if other situations, including the current one, are unwanted), it is usually because a change would be beneficial to someone or something (the speaker, the addressee, other people, institutions, moral principles, etc.). This explains why, quite often, *values* concerning the request plan are asserted (e.g. 'It would probably be easiest...') or discussed (e.g. 'Would that be alright with you?'). Elements of other types might be acknowledged in the Universe of the speaker, referring not to actions, participants, circumstances or values but to specific *meaning-contents* that can be given prominence when isolated as an increment. Thus, 'Just', in (2), does not refer to an entity but brings in the meaning of 'restriction'—here a restriction bearing on the scope of the ultimate goal, in such a way that the request itself is attenuated. Often, the restriction bears directly on the head-action, as in (3).

3.2 Structural distinctions

One issue raised by the last remark is that of dealing with units of different ranks, as boundaries do not always coincide. 'Just / for the week-end //' is related to a verb in a preceding increment ('getting an advance on my paycheck') yet it appears after a *final* pause, as an afterthought. An approach favoring syntax might try to emphasize the relationship with the verb or the clause. A pragmatic alternative (or addition) can be proposed, underlining the fact that speakers (consciously or not) isolate some increments and join others. 'Just' carries the meaning of 'restriction'; giving it prominence through prosody (by separating it both from what precedes and follows it) might therefore be an effective way of increasing the chances of a request to be fulfilled. Indeed, 'Just / for the week-end //' is not verbalized so much for the informational, referential specification it provides concerning the preceding verb, as for the way it restricts the 'cost' of fulfilling the *future* request (of asking for an advance on the salary) and therefore the *present* one ('...tell me who I speak to...').[10] The prosodic boundaries both signal and enact a reorganization of the roles and importance of verbalized elements under pragmatic considerations—a reorganization for which syntactic distinctions fail to account, and which might be erased or downplayed when increments are normalized into 'utterances'.[11]

Still, 'Just' does not function alone. An accurate semantic-pragmatic description should be able to render the facts (a) that signs have meaning in isolation, (b) that they enter in meaningful larger syntactic structures (on which traditional corpus segmentation has focused) and (c) that prosodic cues often cut through these structures or fuse several of them,[12] an operation of (re)organization which is of semantic-pragmatic relevance.

Several types of meaningful units are therefore available.[13] They are treated here on three separate ranks (some of which might require subdivision to cover the whole structural complexity). The semantic ranks describing the verbalized Universe and the verbalizing Manner will commonly deal with whole increments as well as 'sub-increments' (e.g. 'It would probably be easiest' in (1)). The pragmatic ranks (see §3.3), on the other hand, will typically deal with whole increments, as what the speaker *does* through speech seems to be carried out by 'phases' which often fit into increment boundaries (or run over several increments). The general correspondence of phase boundaries with those of increments is strengthened by the observation that when several functions are fulfilled within the limits of one increment, they are usually fulfilled in a *syncretic*, not a successive fashion (though 'phases' may sometimes run on parts of increments only). Focusing on 'functions' of increments leads us to pragmatic distinctions.

3.3 Pragmatic distinctions

The increments uttered when instantiating a request are not just semantically and structurally heterogeneous (some assert judgments, others pinpoint objects or circumstances, etc.), they are also pragmatically heterogeneous: different types of 'phases' fulfilling different functions can usually be distinguished within a request instantiation.[14] Taking each increment one after the other, we can ask: what is the speaker trying to achieve with this increment with regard to the general request under way? do neighboring increments fulfill the same function? are several functions fulfilled by the same increment? if so, can the increment be divided into sub-increments corresponding to different phases, or are all the functions fulfilled syn-

[10] As 'Mr Masry' is the director of the firm, he can be expected to have a say in salary matters, which might influence his reaction to a request to name the office manager.

[11] In other words, this paper believes that functions are fulfilled a bit *below* (with 'phases', see §3.3) and a bit *above* (with 'speech acts', roughly Discourse Units as in Traum and Hinkelman (1992), and see §2) the level of 'utterances'.

[12] In 'Do not smoke in here thank you very much //' (JAW_0h30m49s), fusion of an action-specifying phase with a 'second answer' (which normally follows a *positive* 'first' answer such a 'Ok') expresses the refusal of an alternative.

[13] None of these units need be 'grammatical' in the traditional, syntactic sense, as many types of *fragments* are in fact accepted in spoken language (Goldman-Eisler, 1968).

[14] The labels (e.g. *angling<calling<urging*) are meant to be 'intuitive'. Their pragmatic relevance *vis-à-vis* the formal cues (word order, intonation, etc.) retained to describe speech elements with them is, of course, only assumed for English.

UNIVERSE	(major/head/high/sub/germane/next/ultimate) (mental/physical) ACTION/PROCESS/STATE (P{1-6}); TIME; PLACE; VALUE; 'RESTRICTION';... Notes: Modifiers before action, process or state specify their place on the mental world-map and their type. Modifiers afterwards attribute them to person. At this stage, values are not attributed to person.
MANNER	EGOPHORIC (sends back to speaker); INDEXICAL [INTERPELLATION/POINTING]; DESCRIPTIVE [ASSERTION/QUESTION/EVOCATION/RANGE/(...?) *(of/on)* ACTION/STATE/POSSIBILITY/CIRCUMSTANCE/JUDGMENT/REFLECTION/FEELING/...]; DIRECTIVE[IMPERATIVE/PERFORMATIVE/NOMINAL]; OPERATIVE (performs an action by itself, e.g. 'just', 'please', etc.); (...?) Notes: This level assesses the *semantico-structural* contribution; labels can be modified by 'Ambiguity', which is sometimes part of the speaker's strategy (see Table 3, (1)), and by 'Negative' (*ibid.*, (3)).
PHASES	SPECIFYING/RESTRICTING/QUESTIONING *(of)* MOTIVE/ACTION/GOAL/SCOPE; ANGLING/CALLING/URGING *(for)* ATTENTION/FOCUS/EMPATHY/ACTION; (soft) PHATIC/FOCALIZING/ATTENUATING/MODALIZING/INTENSIFYING/... Notes: This level assesses the *pragmatic* contribution of increments. Label changes are to be expected.
DEPENDENCY	ATTENTION REQUEST; CONFIRMATION REQUEST; METAPRAGMATIC REQUEST;(...?) Notes: Request dependencies are described in Table 3 only when relevant.

Table 2: Preliminary ontology of levels of analysis and their labels (see Table 3 for application)

thetically by the whole increment? if the latter, are the functions distinct (a case represented by sign '&' in Table 3) or is one derived from another (in which case the position on a lower line without '&' represents derivation from functions on a higher line)?

Phases, through their 'vertical' relations with formal manners and their 'horizontal' interrelations, are useful to evaluate request strategies. One important difference between the directive and descriptive manners, for instance, is that in addition to specifying an action, directive manners conventionally convey an urge to enact it. Descriptive manners, as for them, are regularly accompanied by elements fulfilling other functions such as stating the value of the action (1) or questioning its possibility (2). Fine distinctions should also allow to compare, for instance, increments subtly 'angling' for attention (such as the throat clearing in (1)) and others more clearly 'calling' for it (the vocative in (2)), not to forget the cases where obtaining the addressee's attention is presented as a request in itself ('Now you listen' in (3)).

With this last remark, we are hitting upon an important pragmatic distinction: not all increments in a request participate in its instantiation equally. This is not just because different types of 'phases' must be acknowledged but also because, in some cases, these phases actually contribute to the request *via* their participation to the instantiation of a '*satellite*', or '*dependent*' request. True, requests for attention and confirmation are commonly found as 'independent' requests (for instance in a classroom), but they often serve the purpose of ensuring the felicity of a '*main*' request, as in (3). 'Now you listen' and 'You got that?' are requests in their own right;[15] nevertheless, these requests would have no *raison d'être* without the main request not to follow the speaker. A layer can therefore be added in the tables to account for request 'Dependency'; and the head-action of the *main* request gains a new status, as '*major*' action in the request plan.[16]

4 Limitations and prospects

The model presented here has not yet reached a state of maturity where its reliability as an annotation scheme can be tested. Fine-tuning of the distinctions, and clear decision-trees for each rank, are among the next necessary steps. One theoretical limitation is that this approach, in its current form, does not cover the use of metaphoric language and more generally the *lexical* contribution of a number of elements (for instance, the non-professional and vague verb 'to poke around' in (1) is not chosen by chance instead of, say, 'to search for the legal records my firm needs'). As important is the need to take prosody into fuller

[15]The co-speaker's 'Yeah' following the latter is not only an ANSWER but also an AGREEMENT/ACCEPT (or COMMIT), in terms of the SWBD-DAMSL taxonomy (Jurafsky et al., 1997; Stolcke et al., 2000). The general duality affecting 'check questions' was noted in Core and Allen (1997).

[16]Clarification is needed of the Phase/Dependency boundary, i.e. of the criteria used to decide when 'phases' of a request acquire the status of 'dependent request' (of which some uses of 'Come on' and 'Do it' illustrate another type, that of a 'metapragmatic' request to fulfill the main request).

(1)	*Err hmm*	*You know*	*It would probably be easiest*	*if I just squeezed back there and poked around myself*	*Would that be alright with you?*
Universe	-	state (P2)	value	sub-act° + high-act° (P1)	value
Manner	egophoric	descriptive Ambig. Ass°/Q°	descriptive Assert° Judgment	descriptive Evocat° Possibility	descriptive Quest° Judgment
Phases	att° angling	empathy angling	specifying motive & specifying goal		assent angling
	REQUEST (to let speaker go look for files herself)				

(2)	*Mr Masry?*	*(-Yeah)*	*I was wondering*	*can you*	*tell me who I talk to*		*about maybe getting an advance on my paycheck*	*Just*	*for the week-end*
U	addressee		mental proc. (P1)	state (P2)	head-a°	next a° (P1)	ultimate a° (P1)	'restr°'	moment
M	indexical Interpellat°		descriptive Assert° Reflect°	descr. Q° Poss.	descr. Evoc° P.	descr. Evoc° P.	descriptive Evocat° Possib.	operative Restrict°	descr. Evoc° Circ.
Ph	att° calling		soft focalizing & soft modalizing	specifying goal=motive & head-act° specifying & Calling				restricting scope attenuating modalizing	
D	ATTENT° R.	√	REQUEST (to tell speaker how (and if) possible to get advance on her paycheck)						

(3)	*Now*	*you listen*	*I don't give a damn*	*which way you go*	*Just*	*don't follow me*	*You got that?*
Univ.	time	head-act°$_{R'}$	value (feeling)	act° (P2)	'restr°'	major action	sub-action$_{R''}$
Man.	idx.	directive Imp.	descriptive Assertion Feeling	descriptive Range Act°^{s}	operative Restrict°	directive Imp. (neg.)	descriptive Quest° Act°
Ph.	focus angl.	& spec. act° & urging	Expressing concession : modalizing phase :			specifying act° & urging	spec. s-act° & questioning
Dep.	ATTENTION R.		REQUEST FOR ACTION (not to follow speaker)				CONFIRM° R.

Table 3: Description of examples (1), (2) and (3)

account and to include nonverbal cues. Another issue is the fact that repair, backchannel and overlapping tend to be more common in spontaneous speech than in films (work in preparation); these phenomena (all of which can be of pragmatic significance in the context of request-formulation), as well as turn-taking, must be better integrated.

On the plus side, this approach has the advantage of trying to bridge the gap, with strong *empirical* emphasis, between 'emic' parameters such as the speakers' beliefs, desires and intentions, and 'etic' cues from the signifier (Pike, 1954; Blum-Kulka, 1981; Reiss, 1985; Jurafsky, 2004). By focusing on the contribution of increments to the construction of meaning, and by running statistics to reveal which types of increments are used by speakers in which context and according to which concatenation patterns, we should eventually be able to draw a picture of the 'strategies'—conscious or routinized—used when requesting.

5 Conclusion

Traditional speech act theory rests primarily on the structure of isolated sentences. However, at least as far as requests are concerned, speakers tend to express themselves with several increments, heterogeneous both in nature and function. 'Cue-based' approaches designed to *recognize* atomic acts can give accurate descriptions of the speech surface; but the treatment of each unit as 'act' tends to blur the deeper interrelations. The approach presented here, based on the loose inclusion of a lower semantic level under a higher pragmatic level via a structural level, suggests that, as far as the representation of spontaneous spoken language is concerned, gains might be made by broadening the scope of dialogue acts and 'lowering' the aim from the identification of distinct acts to that of the means of their instantiation.

Acknowledgments

I wish to thank Pierre Cotte, Frank Alvarez-Pereyre, Ruth Shalev and an anonymous reviewer for useful comments and discussions.

References

John L. Austin. 1962. *How to do things with words* [edited by J. O. Urmson]. Clarendon Press.

Leonard Bloomfield. 1933. *Language*. Holt & Co.

Shoshana Blum-Kulka. 1981. The study of translation in view of new developments in discourse analysis: The problem of indirect speech acts. *Poetics Today*, 2(4):89–95.

[BRO] *Erin Brockovich*. 2000. Directed by Steven Soderbergh. Written by Susannah Grant. Jersey Films.

Jean Carletta, Amy Isard, Stephen Isard, Jacqueline C. Kowtko, Gwyneth Doherty-Sneddon, Anne H. Anderson. 1997. The Reliability of A Dialogue Structure Coding Scheme. *Computational Linguistics*, 23(1):13–31.

Mark Core and James Allen. 1997. Coding dialogs with the DAMSL annotation scheme. In *Working Notes of the AAAI Fall Symposium on Communicative Action in Humans and Machines*, pages 28–35.

William A. Corsaro. 1977. The clarification request as a feature of adult interactive styles with young children. *Language in Society*, 6:183–207.

[FUG] *The Fugitive*. 1993. Directed by Andrew Davis. Written by Roy Huggins, David Twohy and Jeb Stuart. Warner Bros. Pictures.

Michael L. Geis. 1995. *Speech acts and conversational interaction*. Cambridge University Press.

Frieda Goldman-Eisler. 1968. *Psycholinguistics: Experiments in spontaneous speech*. Academic Press.

H. Paul Grice. 1975. Logic and conversation. In P. Cole and J. Morgan, editors, *Syntax and semantics 3: Speech acts*. Academic Press.

Barbara J. Grosz and Candace L. Sidner. 1986. Attention, intentions, and the structure of discourse. *Computational Linguistics*, 12(3):175–204.

[JAW] *Jaws*. 1975. Directed by Steven Spielberg. Written by Peter Benchley (based on his novel) and Carl Gottlieb. Zanuck/Brown Productions – Universal Pictures.

Daniel Jurafsky, Elizabeth Shriberg and Debra Biasca. 1997. *Switchboard SWBD-DAMSL labeling project coder's manual, Draft 13*. TR 97-02, University of Colorado Institute of Cognitive Science.

Daniel Jurafsky and James H. Martin. 2000. *Speech and language processing: An introduction to natural language processing, computational linguistics, and speech recognition*. Prentice Hall.

Daniel Jurafsky. 2004. Pragmatics and computational linguistics. In L. R. Horn and G. L. Ward, editors, *The handbook of pragmatics*, chapter 26. Blackwell.

Alessandro Lenci. 1994. A relevance-based approach to speech acts. In E. Fava, editor, *Speech acts and linguistic research*. Proceedings of the workshop, July 15–17, 1994, Center of Cognitive Science of New York at Buffalo. Nemo, 1995.

Lori Levin, Ann Thymé-Gobbel, Alon Lavie, Klaus Ries and Klaus Zechner. 1998. A discourse coding scheme for conversational Spanish. In *Proceedings of ICSLP 98*, 6:2335–2338.

C. Raymond Perrault and James F. Allen. 1980. A plan-based analysis of indirect speech acts. *American Journal of Computational Linguistics*, 6:167–182.

Kenneth L. Pike. 1945. *The intonation of American English*. University of Michigan Publications. Reprinted in part as Chapter 3 in D. Bolinger, editor, *Intonation*, Penguin Books, 1972.

Kenneth L. Pike. 1954. *Language in relation to a unified theory of the structure of human behavior*. Summer institute of linguistics.

Matthew Purver, Jonathan Ginzburg and Patrick Healey. 2003. On the means for clarification in dialogue. In J. C. J. Van Kuppevelt and R. W. Smith, editors, *Current and New Directions in Discourse & Dialogue*. Kluwer Academic Publishers.

Matthew Purver. 2004. *The theory and use of clarification requests in dialogue*. Ph.D. thesis. King's College, University of London.

Nira Reiss. 2004. *Speech act taxonomy as a tool for ethnographic description* (Pragmatics and Beyond VI:7). John Benjamins.

Kepa J. Rodríguez and David Schlangen. 2004. Form, intonation and function of clarification requests in German task-oriented spoken dialogues. In *Proceedings of Catalog '04* (The 8th Workshop on the Semantics and Pragmatics of Dialogue, SemDial04), pages 101–108.

John R. Searle. 1969. *Speech acts: An essay in the philosophy of language*. Cambridge University Press.

John R. Searle. 1979. *Expression and meaning: Studies in the theory of speech acts*. Cambridge University Press.

Andreas Stolcke, Klaus Ries, Noah Coccaro, Elizabeth Shriberg, Rebecca Bates, Daniel Jurafsky, Paul Taylor, Rachel Martin, Marie Meteer and Carol Van Ess-Dykema. 2000. Dialog act modeling for automatic tagging and recognition of conversational speech. *Computational linguistics*, 26:98–105.

Michael Stubbs. 1983. *Discourse analysis: The sociolinguistic analysis of natural language* (Language in Society 4). Basil Blackwell Ltd.

David R. Traum and Elizabeth A. Hinkelman. 1992. Conversation acts in task-oriented spoken dialogue. *Computational Intelligence*, 8(3):575–599.

Identifying Segment Topics in Medical Dictations

Johannes Matiasek, Jeremy Jancsary
Alexandra Klein
Austrian Research Institute for
Artificial Intelligence
Freyung 6, Wien, Austria
`firstname.lastname@ofai.at`

Harald Trost
Department of Medical Cybernetics
and Artificial Intelligence
of the Center for Brain Research,
Medical University Vienna, Austria
`harald.trost@meduniwien.ac.at`

Abstract

In this paper, we describe the use of lexical and semantic features for topic classification in dictated medical reports. First, we employ SVM classification to assign whole reports to coarse work-type categories. Afterwards, text segments and their topic are identified in the output of automatic speech recognition. This is done by assigning work-type-specific topic labels to each word based on features extracted from a sliding context window, again using SVM classification utilizing semantic features. Classifier stacking is then used for a posteriori error correction, yielding a further improvement in classification accuracy.

1 Introduction

The use of automatic speech recognition (ASR) is quite common in the medical domain, where for every consultation or medical treatment a written report has to be produced. Usually, these reports are dictated and transcribed afterwards. The use of ASR can, thereby, significantly reduce the typing efforts, but, as can be seen in figure 1, quite some work is left.

```
complaint dehydration weakness and diarrhea full
stop Mr.  Will Shawn is a 81-year-old cold Asian
gentleman who came in with fever and Persian
diaper was sent to the emergency department by his
primary care physician due him being dehydrated
period ... neck physical exam general alert and
oriented times three known acute distress vital
signs are stable ... diagnosis is one chronic
diarrhea with hydration he also has hypokalemia
neck number thromboctopenia probably duty liver
cirrhosis ... a plan was discussed with patient in
detail will transfer him to a nurse and facility
for further care ... end of dictation
```

Figure 1: Raw output of speech recognition

When properly edited and formatted, the same dictation appears significantly more comprehensible, as can be seen in figure 2.

```
CHIEF COMPLAINT
Dehydration, weakness and diarrhea.

HISTORY OF PRESENT ILLNESS
Mr.  Wilson is a 81-year-old Caucasian gentleman
who came in here with fever and persistent
diarrhea.  He was sent to the emergency department
by his primary care physician due to him being
dehydrated.
...
PHYSICAL EXAMINATION
  GENERAL: He is alert and oriented times three,
     not in acute distress.

  VITAL SIGNS: Stable.
...

DIAGNOSIS
  1. Chronic diarrhea with dehydration.  He also
     has hypokalemia.
  2. Thromboctopenia, probably due to liver
     cirrhosis.
...
PLAN AND DISCUSSION
The plan was discussed with the patient in detail.
Will transfer him to a nursing facility for
further care.
...
```

Figure 2: A typical medical report

Besides the usual problem with recognition errors, section headers are often not dictated or hard to recognize as such. One task that has to be performed in order to arrive at the structured report shown in figure 2 is therefore to identify topical sections in the text and to classify them accordingly.

In the following, we first describe the problem setup, the steps needed for data preparation, and the division of the classification task into subproblems. We then describe the experiments performed and their results.

In the outlook we hint at ways to integrate this approach with another, multilevel, segmentation framework.

2 Data Description and Problem Setup

Available corpus data consists of raw recognition results and manually formatted and corrected reports of medical dictations. 11462 reports were

Proceedings of EACL 2009 Workshop on Semantic Representation of Spoken Language - SRSL 2009, pages 19–25,
Athens, Greece, 30 March 2009.

available in both forms, 51382 reports only as corrected transcripts. When analysing the data, it became clear that the structure of segment topics varied strongly across different work-types. Thus we decided to pursue a two-step approach: firstly classify reports according to their work-type and, secondly, train and apply work-type specific classification models for segment topic classification.

2.1 Classification framework

For all classification tasks discussed here, we employed support-vector machines (SVM, Vapnik (1995)) as the statistical framework, though in different incarnations and setups. SVMs have proven to be an effective means for text categorization (Joachims, 1998) as they are capable to robustly deal with high-dimensional, sparse feature spaces. Depending on the task, we experimented with different feature weighting schemes and SVM kernel functions as will be described in section 3.

2.2 Features used for classification

The usual approach in text categorization is to use bag-of-word features, i.e. the words occuring in a document are collected disregarding the order of their appearance. In the domain of medical dictation, however, often abbreviations or different medical terms may be used to refer to the same semantic concept. In addition, medical terms often are multi-word expressions, e.g., "coronary heart disease". Therefore, a better approach for feature mapping is needed to arrive at features at an appropriate generalization level:

- Tokenization is performed using a large finite-state lexicon including multi-word medical concepts extracted from the UMLS medical metathesaurus (Lindberg et al., 1993). Thus, multi-word terms remain intact. In addition, numeric quantities in special (spoken or written) formats or together with a dimension are mapped to semantic types (e.g. "blood pressure" or "physical quantity"), also using a finite-state transducer.

- The tokens are lemmatized and, if possible, replaced by the UMLS *semantic concept* identifier(s) they map to. Thus, "CHD", "coronary disease" and "coronary heart disease" all map to the same concept "C0010068".

- In addition, also the UMLS *semantic type*, if available, is used as a feature, so, in the example above, "B2.2.1.2.1" (Disease or Syndrome) is added.

- Since topics in a medical report roughly follow an order, for the segment topic identification task also the relative position of a word in the report (ranging from -1 to +1) is used.

We also explored different weighting schemes:

- **binary**: only the presence of a feature is indicated.

- **term frequency**: the number of occurences of a feature in the segment to be classified is used as weight.

- **TFIDF**: a measure popular from information retrieval, where $tfidf_{i,j}$ of term t_i in document $d_j \in D$ is usually defined as

$$\frac{\mathrm{ct}_{i,j}}{\sum_i \mathrm{ct}_{i,j}} \cdot \log \frac{|D|}{|\{d_j : t_i \in d_j\}|}$$

An example of how this feature extraction process works is given below:

token(s)	feature(s)	comment
...		
an		*stop word*
78 year old	QH_OLD	*pattern-based type*
female	C0085287	*UMLS concept*
	A2.9.2	*UMLS semtype*
intubated	intubate	*lemmatized (no concept)*
with		*stop word*
lung cancer	C0242379	*UMLS concept*
	C0684249	*UMLS concept*
	B2.2.1.2.1.2	*UMLS semtype*
...		

2.3 Data Annotation

For the first classification task, i.e. work-type classification, no further annotation is necessary, every report in our data corpus had a label indicating the work-type. For the segment topic classification task, however, every token of the report had to be assigned a topic label.

2.3.1 Analysis of Corrected Transcripts

For the experiments described here, we concentrated on the "Consultations" work-type, for which clear structuring recommendations, such as E2184-02 (ASTM International, 2002), exist. However, in practice the structure of medical reports shows high variation and deviations from the guidelines, making it harder to come up with an appropriate set of class labels. Therefore, using the aforementioned standard, we assigned the headings that actually appeared in the data to the closest type, introducing new types only when absolutely necessary. Thus we arrived at 23 heading classes. Every (possibly multi-word) token was then labeled with the heading class of the last section heading occurring before it in the text using a simple parser.

2.3.2 Aligment and Label Transfer

When inspecting manually corrected reports (cf. fig. 2), one can easily identify a heading and classify the topic of the text below it accordingly. However, our goal is to develop a model for identifying and classifying segments in the *dictation*, thus we have to map the annotation of corrected reports onto the corresponding ASR output. The basic idea here is to align the tokens of the corrected report with the tokens in ASR output and to copy the annotations (cf. figure 3). There are some problems we have to take care of during alignment:

1. non-dictated items in the corrected test (e.g. punctuation, headings)
2. dictated words that do not occur in the corrected text (meta instructions, repetitions)
3. non-identical but corresponding items (recognition errors, reformulations)

For this alignment task, a standard string-edit distance based method is not sufficient. Therefore, we augment it with a more sophisticated cost function. It assigns tokens that are similar (either from a semantic or from a phonetic point of view) a low cost for substitution, whereas dissimilar tokens receive a prohibitively expensive score. Costs for deletion and insertion are assigned inversely. Semantic similarity is computed using Wordnet (Fellbaum, 1998) and UMLS. For phonetic matching, the Metaphone algorithm (Philips, 1990) was used (for details see Huber et al. (2006) and Jancsary et al. (2007)).

3 Experiments

3.1 Work-Type Categorization

In total we had 62844 written medical reports with assigned work-type information from different hospitals, 7 work-types are distinguished. We randomly selected approximately a quarter of the

corrected report		OP	ASR output	
...	...	...	...	...
ChiefCompl	CHIEF	del		
ChiefCompl	COMPLAINT	sub	complaint	ChiefCompl
ChiefCompl	Dehydration	sub	dehydration	ChiefCompl
ChiefCompl	,	del		
ChiefCompl	weakness	sub	weakness	ChiefCompl
ChiefCompl	and	sub	and	ChiefCompl
ChiefCompl	diarrhea	sub	diarrhea	ChiefCompl
ChiefCompl	.	sub	fullstop	ChiefCompl
HistoryOfP	Mr.	sub	Mr.	HistoryOfP
HistoryOfP	Wilson	sub	Will	HistoryOfP
		ins	Shawn	HistoryOfP
HistoryOfP	is	sub	is	HistoryOfP
HistoryOfP	a	sub	a	HistoryOfP
HistoryOfP	81-year-old	sub	81-year-old	HistoryOfP
HistoryOfP	Caucasian	sub	cold	HistoryOfP
HistoryOfP		ins	Asian	HistoryOfP
HistoryOfP	gentleman	sub	gentleman	HistoryOfP
HistoryOfP	who	sub	who	HistoryOfP
HistoryOfP	came	sub	came	HistoryOfP
HistoryOfP	in	del		
HistoryOfP	here	sub	here	HistoryOfP
HistoryOfP	with	sub	with	HistoryOfP
HistoryOfP	fever	sub	fever	HistoryOfP
HistoryOfP	and	sub	and	HistoryOfP
HistoryOfP	persistent	sub	Persian	HistoryOfP
HistoryOfP	diarrhea	sub	diaper	HistoryOfP
HistoryOfP	.	del		
...	...	...	...	...

Figure 3: Mapping labels via alignment

reports as the training set, the rest was used for testing. The distribution of the data can be seen in table 1.

Trainingset		Testset		Work-Type
649	4.1	1966	4.2	CA Cardiology
7965	51.0	24151	51.1	CL ClinicalReports
1867	11.9	5590	11.8	CN Consultations
1120	7.2	3319	7.0	DS DischargeSummaries
335	2.1	878	1.8	ER EmergencyMedicine
2185	14.0	6789	14.4	HP HistoryAndPhysicals
1496	9.6	4534	9.6	OR OperativeReports
15617		47227		Total

Table 1: Distribution of Work-types

As features for categorization, we used a bag-of-words approach, but instead of the surface form of every token of a report, we used its semantic features as described in section 2.2. As a categorization engine, we used LIBSVM (Chang&Lin, 2001) with an RBF kernel. The features where weighted with TFIDF. In order to compensate for different document length, each feature vector was normalized to unit length. After some parameter tuning iterations, the SVM model performs really well with a microaveraged F1[1] value of 0.9437. This indicates high overall accuracy, and the macroaveraged F1 value of 0.9341 shows, that also lower frequency categories are predicted quite reliably. The detailed results are shown in table 2.

Thus the first step in the cascaded model, i.e. the selection of the work-type specific segment

[1] $F1 = \frac{2 \times precision \times recall}{precision + recall}$

	predicted								rec.	prec.	F1
true		CA	CL	CN	DS	ER	HP	OR			
CA	1966	1882	53	5	6	0	9	11	0.9573	0.9787	0.9679
CL	24151	25	23675	217	13	18	155	48	0.9803	0.9529	0.9664
CN	5590	1	447	4695	7	17	413	10	0.8399	0.8814	0.8601
DS	3319	1	37	8	3241	2	27	3	0.9765	0.9818	0.9792
ER	878	0	90	7	10	754	13	4	0.8588	0.9425	0.8987
HP	6789	4	512	393	22	7	5838	13	0.8599	0.9040	0.8814
OR	4534	10	31	2	2	2	3	4484	0.9890	0.9805	0.9847
										microaveraged	**0.9437**
										macroaveraged	**0.9341**

Table 2: Work-Type categorization results

topic model, yields reliable performance.

3.2 Segment Topic Classification

In contrast to work-type categorization, where whole reports need to be categorized, the identification of segment topics requires a different setup. Since not only the topic labels are to be determined, but also segment boundaries are unknown in the classification task, *each token* constitutes an example under this setting. Segments are then contiguous text regions with the same topic label. It is clearly not enough to consider only features of the token to be classified, thus we include also contextual and positional features.

3.2.1 Feature and Kernel Selection

In particular, we employ a sliding window approach, i.e. for each data set not only the token to be classified, but also the 10 preceding and the 10 following tokens are considered (at the beginning or towards the end of a report, context is reduced appropriately). This window defines the text fragment to be used for classifying the center token, and features are collected from this window again as described in section 2.2. Additionaly, the relative position (ranging from -1 to +1) of the center token is used as a feature.

The rationale behind this setup is that

1. usually topics in medical reports follow an ordering, thus relative position may help.

2. holding features also from adjacent segments might also be helpful since topic succession also follows typical patterns.

3. a sufficiently sized context might also smooth label assignment and prevent label oscillation, since the classification features for adjacent words overlap to a great deal.

A second choice to be made was the selection of the kernel best suited for this particular classification problem. In order to get an impression, we made a preliminary mini-experiment with just 5 reports each for training (4341 datasets) and testing (3382 datasets), the results of which are reported in table 3.

	Accuracy	
Feature Weight	linear	RBF
TFIDF	0.4977	0.3131
TFIDF normalized	0.5544	0.6199
Binary	0.6417	0.6562

Table 3: Preliminary Kernel Comparison

While these results are of course not significant, two things could be learned from the preliminary experiment:

1. linear kernels may have similar or even better performance,

2. training times with LIBSVM with a large number of examples may soon get infeasible (we were not able to repeat this experiment with 50 reports due to excessive runtime).

Since LibSVM solves linear and nonlinear SVMs in the same way, LibSVM is not particularly efficient for linear SVMs. Therefore we decided to switch to Liblinear (Fan et al., 2008), a linear classifier optimized for handling data with millions of instances and features[2].

[2]Indeed, training a model from 669 reports (463994 examples) could be done in less then 5 minutes!

#	True Label	Total	F1	predicted class label (#)					
				...	3	4	...	14	...
	...	...	...	...	...	...	...	...	...
3	Diagnosis	40871	0.603	...	24391	2864	...	8691	...
4	DiagAndPlan	21762	0.365	...	5479	6477	...	7950	...
	...	...	...	...	...	...	...	...	...
14	Plan	31729	0.598	...	5714	3419	...	21034	...
	...	...	...	...	...	...	...	...	...

Table 4: Confusion matrix (part of)

3.2.2 Segment Topic Classification Results

Experiments were performed on a randomly selected subset of reports from the "Consultations" work-type (1338) that were available both in corrected form and in raw ASR output form. Annotations were constructed for the corrected transcripts, as described in section 2.3, transfer of labels to the ASR output was performed as shown in section 2.3.2.

Both data sets were split into training and test sets of equal size (669 reports each), experiments with different feature weighting schemes have been performed on both corrected data and ASR output. The overall results are shown in table 5.

Feature weights	corrected reports		ASR output	
	micro-avg.F1	macro-avg.F1	micro-avg.F1	macro-avg.F1
TFIDF	0.7553	**0.5178**	0.7136	**0.4440**
TFIDF norm.	0.7632	0.3470	0.7268	0.3131
Binary	**0.7693**	0.4636	**0.7413**	0.3953

Table 5: Segment topic classification results

Consistently, macroaveraged F1 values are much lower than their microaveraged counterparts indicating that low-frequency topic labels are predicted with less accuracy.

Also, segment classification works better with corrected reports than with raw ASR output. The reason for that behaviour is

1. ASR data are more noisy due to recognition errors, and

2. while in corrected reports appropriate section headers are available (not as header, but the words) this is not necessarily the case in ASR output (also the wording of dictated headers and written headers may be different).

A general note on the used topic labels must also be made: Due to the nature of our data it was inevitable to use topic labels that overlap in some cases. The most prominent example here is "*Diagnosis*", "*Plan*", and "*Diagnosis and Plan*". The third label clearly subsumes the other two, but in the data available the physicians often decided to dictate diagnoses and the respective treatment in an alternating way, associating each diagnosis with the appropriate plan. This made it necessary to include all three labels, with obvious effects that could easily seen when inspecting the confusion matrix, a part of which is shown in table 4.

When looking at the misclassifications in these 3 categories it can easily be seen, that they are predominantly due to overlapping categories.

Another source of problems in the data is the skewed distribution of segment types in the reports. Sections labelled with one of the four label categories that weren't predicted at all (*ChiefComplaints*, *Course*, *Procedure*, and *Time*, cf. table 6) occur in less than 2% of the reports or are infrequent and extremely short. This fact had, of course, undesirable effects on the macroavered F1 scores. Additional difficulties that are similar to the overlap problem discussed above are strong thematic similarities between some section types (e.g., *Findings* and *Diagnosis*, or *ReasonForEncounter* and *HistoryOfPresentIllness*) that result in a very similar vocabulary used.

Given these difficulties due to the data, the results are encouraging. There is, however, still plenty of room left for improvement.

3.3 Improving Topic Classification

Liblinear does not only provide class label predictions, it is also possible to obtain class probabilities. The usual way then to predict the label is to choose the one with the highest probability. When analysing the errors made by the segment topic classification task described above, it turned out that often the correct label was ranked second or third (cf. table 6). Thus, the idea of just taking

Label	count	correct prediction in best	best 2	best 3
Allergies	3456	29.72	71.64	85.21
ChiefComplai	697			
Course	30			
Diagnosis	43565	64.69	83.29	91.37
DiagAndPlan	19409	35.24	70.45	86.81
DiagnosticSt	35554	82.47	91.34	93.05
Findings	791		0.38	1.26
Habits	2735	7.31	32.69	41.76
HistoryOfPre	122735	92.26	97.55	98.20
Medication	14553	85.87	93.38	95.22
Neurologic	5226	54.08	86.93	89.19
PastHistory	43775	71.13	86.26	88.82
PastSurgical	5752	49.32	78.88	84.47
PhysicalExam	86031	93.56	97.01	97.57
Plan	36476	62.57	84.63	94.65
Practitioner	1262	55.07	76.78	82.73
Procedures	109			
ReasonForEnc	15819	25.42	42.35	43.47
ReviewOfSyst	29316	79.81	89.90	91.87
Time	58			
Total	467349	76.93	88.65	92.00

Table 6: Ranked predictions

	True Label		Predicted	Label probabilities (%) ...	10	11	12	...	17	18
	...									
=	PastHistory [11]	age	PastHistory		0	95	0		0	0
=	PastHistory [11]	63	PastHistory		0	95	0		0	0
=	PastHistory [11]	and	PastHistory		0	95	0		0	1
=	PastHistory [11]	his	PastHistory		0	95	0		0	1
=	PastHistory [11]	father	PastHistory		0	88	0		0	9
=	PastHistory [11]	died	PastHistory		0	90	0		0	8
=	PastHistory [11]	from	PastHistory		0	84	0		0	14
=	PastHistory [11]	myocardial infa	PastHistory		0	81	0		0	17
=	PastHistory [11]	at	PastHistory		0	77	0		0	20
=	PastHistory [11]	age	PastHistory		0	78	0		1	19
=	PastHistory [11]	57	PastHistory		0	78	0		1	19
=	PastHistory [11]	period	PastHistory		0	78	0		1	19
-	ReviewOfSyst[18]	review	PastHistory		0	76	0		1	20
-	ReviewOfSyst[18]	of	PastHistory		0	76	0		1	21
-	ReviewOfSyst[18]	systems	PastHistory		0	78	0		0	19
-	ReviewOfSyst[18]	he	PastHistory		1	57	0		1	37
=	ReviewOfSyst[18]	has	ReviewOfSyst		1	32	0		1	58
=	ReviewOfSyst[18]	had	ReviewOfSyst		1	32	0		1	58
-	ReviewOfSyst[18]	progressive	PastHistory		1	49	0		1	42
-	ReviewOfSyst[18]	weight loss	PastHistory		1	60	0		1	32
=	ReviewOfSyst[18]	period	ReviewOfSyst		1	31	0		0	62
=	ReviewOfSyst[18]	his	ReviewOfSyst		1	13	0		1	81
=	ReviewOfSyst[18]	appetite	ReviewOfSyst		1	13	0		1	81
	...									

Figure 4: predicted label probabilites

the highest ranked class label could be possibly improved by a more informed choice.

While the segment topic classifier already takes contextual features into account, it has still no information on the classification results of the neighboring text segments. However, there are constraints on the length of text segments, thus, e.g. a text segment of length 1 with a different topic label than the surrounding text is highly implausible. Furthermore, there are also regularities in the succession of topic labels, which can be captured by the monostratal local classification only indirectly – if at all.

A look at figure 4 exemplifies how a better informed choice of the label could result in higher prediction accuracy. The segment labelled "*PastHistory*" correctly ends 4 tokens earlier than predicted, and, additionally, this label erroneously is predicted again for the phrase "*progressive weight loss*". The correct label, however, has still a rather high probability in the predicted label distribution. By means of stacking an additional classier onto the first one we hope to be able to correct some of the locally made errors a posteriori.

The setup for the error correction classifier we experimented with was as follows (it was performed only for the segment topic classifier trained on ASR output with binary feature weights):

1. The *training* set of the classifier was classified, and the predicted label probabilities were collected as features.

2. Again, a sliding window (with different sizes) was used for feature construction. Features were set up for each label at each window position and the respective predicted label probability was used as its value.

3. A linear classifier was trained on these features of the training set

4. This classifier was applied to the results of classifying the test set with the original segment topic classifier.

Three different window sizes were used on the corrected reports, only one window was applied on ASR output (cf. table 7). As can be seen, each

context window	corrected reports micro-avg.F1	corrected reports macro-avg.F1	ASR output micro-avg.F1	ASR output macro-avg.F1
No correction	0.7693	0.4636	0.7413	0.3953
$[-3, +3]$	0.7782	0.4773	-	-
$[-6, +0]$	0.7798	0.4754	-	-
$[-3, +4]$	0.7788	0.4769	0.7520	0.4055

Table 7: A posteriori correction results

context variant improved on both microaveraged and macroaveraged F1 in a range of 0,9 to 1.4 percent points. Thus, stacked error correction indeed is possible and able to improve classification results.

4 Conclusion and Outlook

We have presented a 3 step approach to segment topic identification in dictations of medical reports. In the first step, a categorization of work-type is performed on the whole report using SVM classification employing semantic features. The categorization model yields good performance (over 94% accuracy) and is a prerequisite for subsequent application of work-type specific segment classification models.

For segment topic detection, every word was assigned a class label based on contextual features in a sliding window approach. Here also semantic features were used as a means for feature generalisation. In various experiments, linear models using binary feature weights had the best performance. A posteriori error correction via classifier stacking additionally improved the results.

When comparing our results to the results of Jancsary et al. (2008), who pursue a multi-level segmentation aproach using conditional random fields optimizing over the whole report, the locally obtained SVM results cannot compete fully. On label chain 2, which is equivalent to segment topics as investigated here, Jancsary et al. (2008) report an estimated accuracy of 81.45 ± 2.14 % on ASR output (after some postprocessing), whereas our results, even with a posteriori error correction, are at least 4 percent points behind. This is probably due to the fact that the multi-level annotation employed in Jancsary et al. (2008) contains additional information useful for the learning task, and constraints between the levels improve segmentation behavior at the segment boundaries. Nevertheless, our approach has the merit of employing a framework that can be trained in a fraction of the time needed for CRF training, and classification works locally.

An investigation on how to combine these two complementary approaches is planned for the future. The idea here is to use the probability distributions on labels returned by our approach as (additional) features in the CRF model. It might be possible to leave out some other features currently employed in return, thereby reducing model complexity. The benefit we hope to get by doing so are shorter training time for CRF training, and, since, contrary to CRFs, SVMs are a large margin classification method, hopefully the CRF model can be improved by the present approach.

Acknowledgments

The work presented here has been carried out in the context of the Austrian KNet competence network COAST. We gratefully acknowledge funding by the Austrian Federal Ministry of Economics and Labour, and ZIT Zentrum fuer Innovation und Technologie, Vienna. The Austrian Research Institute for Artificial Intelligence is supported by the Austrian Federal Ministry for Transport, Innovation, and Technology and by the Austrian Federal Ministry for Science and Research.

References

ASTM International. 2002. ASTM E2184-02: Standard specification for healthcare document formats.

C.-C. Chang and C.-J. Lin. 2001. LIBSVM: a library for support vector machines. Software available at http://www.csie.ntu.edu.tw/ cjlin/libsvm

R.-E. Fan, K.-W. Chang, C.-J. Hsieh, X.-R. Wang, and C.-J. Lin. 2008. LIBLINEAR: A library for large linear classification. *Journal of Machine Learning Research*, 9(2008):1871–1874.

C. Fellbaum. 1998. *WordNet: an electronic lexical database*. MIT Press, Cambridge, MA.

M. Huber, J. Jancsary, A. Klein, J. Matiasek, H. Trost. 2006. Mismatch interpretation by semantics-driven alignment. *Proceedings of Konvens 2006*.

J. Jancsary, A. Klein, J. Matiasek, H. Trost. 2007. Semantics-based Automatic Literal Reconstruction Of Dictations. In Alcantara M. and Declerck T.(eds.), *Semantic Representation of Spoken Language 2007 (SRSL7)* Universidad de Salamanca, Spain, pp. 67-74.

J. Jancsary, J. Matiasek, H. Trost. 2008. Revealing the Structure of Medical Dictations with Conditional Random Fields. Proceedings of the 2008 Conference on Empirical Methods in Natural Language Processing. Association for Computational Linguistics, pp. 1–10.

T. Joachims. 1998. Text Categorization with Support Vector Machines: Learning with Many Relevant Features. Proceedings of the European Conference on Machine Learning. Springer, pp. 137–142.

D.A.B. Lindberg, B.L. Humphreys, A.T. McCray. 1993. The Unified Medical Language System. *Methods of Information in Medicine*, (32):281-291.

Lawrence Philips. 1990. Hanging on the metaphone. *Computer Language*, 7(12).

V.N. Vapnik 1995. *The Nature of Statistical Learning Theory*. Springer.

Semantic Representation of Non-Sentential Utterances in Dialog

Silvie Cinková
Charles University in Prague
Faculty of Mathematics and Physics
Institute of Formal and Applied Linguistics
Malostranské náměstí 25
CZ-118 00 Praha 1
`cinkova@ufal.mff.cuni.cz`

Abstract

Being confronted with spontaneous speech, our current annotation scheme requires alterations that would reflect the abundant use of non-sentential fragments with clausal meaning tightly connected to their context, which do not systematically occur in written texts. The purpose of this paper is to list the common patterns of non-sentential fragments and their contexts and to find a smooth resolution of their semantic annotation.

1 Introduction

Spontaneous speech, even assuming a perfect ASR, is hard to parse because of the enormous occurrence of disfluencies and syntactic deviations. Some disfluencies can be regarded as speaker's errors, which are being corrected or remain uncorrected during the speaker's turn. Such disfluencies are e.g.:

- stammering (`We w-went there to-together`)
- restart with or without an interregnum (`John no sorry Jane was there, too`)
- repetitions (`So you like you like drinking`)
- hesitation sounds, long silence, fillers, filler phrases, etc. (`EH so ... you kinda like you know HMM drinking`)

In NLP, such disfluencies can be removed before any syntactic or semantic processing since they cause confusion without adding any semantic information. In machine-learning tasks, disfluency is sought to be automatically removed by learning from disfluency-marked corpora or corpora of text edits (Hajič et al., 2008; Fitzgerald and Jelinek, 2008) to smooth the input text into written-language standard before parsing.

On the other hand, there is another sort of disfluencies, which do not disturb the course of the dialog, namely contextual ellipsis: even though most people remember being taught at school to answer questions with a complete sentence, not even educated speakers performing a sophisticated dialog always do so, and yet they do not sound incorrect. Clearly, an extensive use of ellipsis is an inherent feature of verbal interaction between speakers, which is usually smoothly perceived by the listener and thus all right in its place.

Such "fragmentary utterances that do not have the form of a full sentence according to most traditional grammars, but that nevertheless convey a complete clausal meaning" are called **non-sentential utterances (NSUs)**[1]. A consistent reconstruction of their clausal meaning is inevitable for any semantic representation of dialogs. The present paper describes a tentative semantic representation of NSUs in the Functional Generative Description (FGD) framework (Sgall et al., 1986).

[1] The term NSU as well as its definition comes from Fernández et al., 2007.

Proceedings of EACL 2009 Workshop on Semantic Representation of Spoken Language - SRSL 2009, pages 26–33, Athens, Greece, 30 March 2009.

2 NSUs in PhotoPal Dialogs

2.1 NSU taxonomy

Fernández et al. (2007) introduce a taxonomy of NSUs based on the dialog transcripts from BNC (Burnard, 2000). They stress that NSUs are not limited to question-answer pairs but can appear as responses to any preceding utterance. Our observations confirm this. NSUs are highly ambiguous without context. Consider the following example:

```
A: I left it on the table.
B: On the table.
```
I confirm/I understand what you say: you left it on the table.

```
A: Where did you leave it?
B: On the table.
```
I answer your question: I left it on the table.

```
A: I think I put it er...
B: On the table.
```
I know in advance what you want to say or what you would want to say if you knew that.

```
A: Should I put it back on the shelf?
B: On the table.
```
No, don't put it back on the shelf, but put it on the table instead.

If reconstructed into a complete sentence, the NSU would get different shapes in the respective contexts (see the paraphrases in italics).

The NSU taxonomy proposed by Fernández et al. (2007) divides the NSUs into 15 classes:

- Clarification Ellipsis (`Two people` *[did you say were there]*`?`)
- Check Question (`[...]Okay?`)
- Reprise Sluice (`What`*[did you say]*`?`)
- Direct Sluice (`What?/Who?/When?`)
- Short Answer [to wh-question] (`My Aunty Peggy.`)
- Plain Affirmative Answer / Rejection (`Yes. / No.`)
- Repeated Affirmative Answer (`Very loud, yes.`)
- Helpful Rejection (`No, Billy.`)
- Plain Acknowledgement (`Mhm.`)
- Repeated Acknowledgement (part of the preceding segment repeated)
- Propositional and Factual Modifiers (`Probably not. / Oh, great!`)
- Bare Modifier Phrase (adjuncts modifying a contextual utterance)
- Conjunct (fragments introduced by conjunctions)
- Filler (fragments filling a gap left by a previous unfinished utterance)

2.2 PhotoPal Dialog Corpora

Our goal is semantically annotated spoken conversations between two speakers over a family album. One English corpus (NAP) and one Czech corpus have been built within the Companions project (www.companions-project.org) as gold-standard data for a machine-learning based dialog system ("PhotoPal") that should be able to handle a natural-like conversation with a human user, helping to sort the user's photographs and encouraging the user to reminisce. The PhotoPal is supposed to keep track of the mentioned entities as well as to make some inferences.

The NAP corpus (Bradley et al., 2008) comprises about 200k tokens of literal manual transcriptions of audio recordings, which are interlinked with a multiple disfluency annotation (Cinková et al., 2008). The Czech PhotoPal corpus is still growing (Hajič et al., 2009), comprising about 200k tokens at the moment (including double annotation).

To ease the understanding, all authentic corpus examples will be taken from the English NAP corpus. However, most examples in this paper are taken from Fernández et al. (2007) and modified when needed to illustrate a contrast.

3 Semantic representation of NAP NSUs

3.1 Functional Generative Description

The Functional Generative Description (FGD) is a stratified formal language description based on the structuralist tradition, developed since the

1960's. The unique contribution of FGD is the so-called tectogrammatical representation (TR). It is being implemented in a family of semantically annotated treebanks.

3.2 Tectogrammatical Representation

Being conceived as an underlying syntactic representation, the TR captures the linguistic meaning of the sentence, which is its basic description unit. In the TR annotation, each sentence is represented as a projective dependency tree with nodes and edges. The attribute values include references to the analytical (surface-syntax) layer. Only content words are represented by nodes. Function words are represented as attribute values. Each node has a semantic label ("functor"), which renders the semantic relation of the given node to its parent node. The TR annotation captures the following aspects of text:

- syntactic and semantic dependencies
- argument structure (data interlinked with a lexicon)
- information structure (topic-focus articulation)
- grammatical and contextual coreference
- ellipsis restoration.

Fig. 1 shows a sentence with restored ellipsis. The elided predicate in the second conjunct was copied from the first conjunct predicate (copied and generated nodes have square shape).

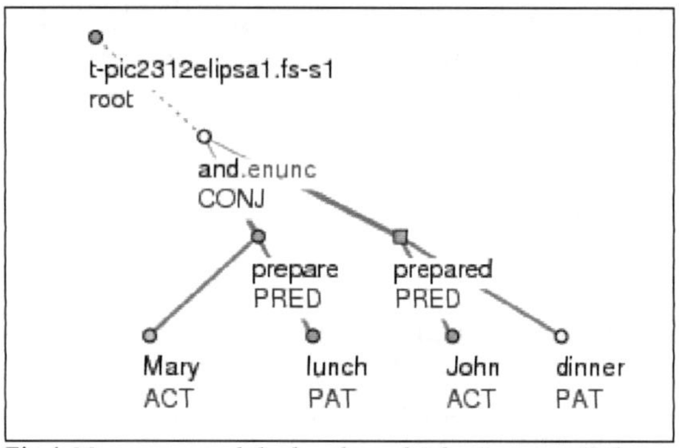

Fig.1 *Mary prepared the lunch, and John [prepared] the dinner.*

3.3 Ellipsis Restoration and Contextual Coreference

Assumingly, any tectogrammatical representation of NSUs is about the most appropriate resolution of contextual ellipsis and coreference.
TR distinguishes two types of ellipsis:

- contextual ellipsis, i.e. ellipsis occurring when the lexical content of the omitted element is clear from the context and easily recoverable. The speaker omitted this element, since he considered its repetition unnecessary.
- grammatical ellipsis, i.e. such ellipsis that occurs when the elided element cannot appear on the surface for grammatical reasons but is cognitively present in the meaning of the utterance (e.g. the unexpressed subject of controlled infinitives).

Every occurrence of a given verb must correspond to the appropriate lexicon frame. Any obligatory arguments missing must be filled in as node substitutes even if the node could be copied from the context. The substitutes have special lemmas according to their function.

Fig. 2 illustrates a contextual ellipsis of a dependent node. The tree represents the answer: `He has [wrapped the book]` to the question: `Has the shop assistant wrapped the book?` In fact, the tree renders the sentence `He has`. To complete the argument structure frame of the verb `wrap`, the node `book` with the Patient semantic label is inserted into the frame in form of a node with the t-lemma substitute for personal pronoun (`#PersPron`, square node) exactly in the same way as the expressed `he`. The node-constituting lexical verb `wrap` is copied from the previous sentence as a square node while `has` becomes its attribute value, since it is an auxiliary verb. The subject `He` is only converted into the `#PersPron` substitute (with appropriate values inside).

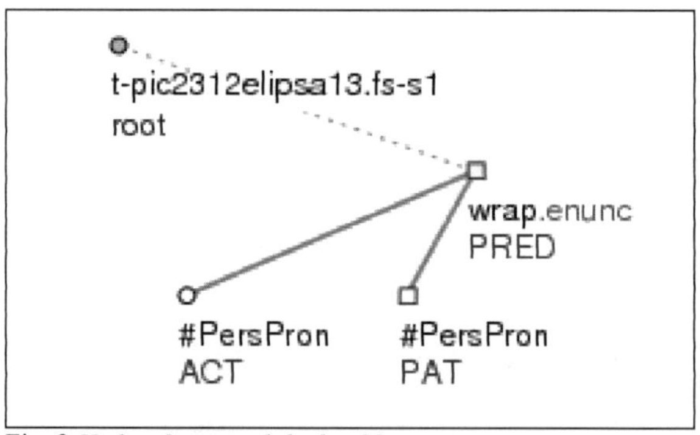

Fig. 2 *He has [wrapped the book].*

In the complete TR annotation, a contextual-coreference arrow would lead from the

#PersPron nodes to their antecedent nodes in the previous sentence (to assistant and book, respectively).

3.4 Basic Principles of NSU Representation in TR

The effort to reconstruct the clausal meaning of non-sentential utterances was motivated by the following basic assumptions:

- The text contains utterance-response pairs.
- NSU is the response to an utterance U[2].
- The utterance U has a finite-verb predicate UPred with or without modifiers (arguments and adjuncts) UMods, which can be assigned functors.
- Even UPred can be an elided predicate.
- All NSUs (except interjections but incl. plain yes and no) contain an implicit (elided) predicate NSUPred. NSUPred is either identical with UPred, or it is an unknown verb, but we can imagine how it relates NSU and U.
- NSU can be attached to a finite clause.
- NSU inherits UPred along with all UMods.
- When there is a semantic conflict, NSUMods overrule the inherited implicit UMods in NSU (repetition is also regarded as conflict).
- NSUMod overrules UMod in the highest position possible in the subtree.

3.5 TR Representation Elements for NSU

This annotation introduced a new category into the annotation scheme. We called the category response_type and designed it in the same way as the coreference annotation. It is visualized as arrows of various colors pointing from NSUMod to UMod. Each type is indicated by a different color.

The utterance-response pair consists of two parts: the antecedent utterance U and the response NSU. The finite verb predicate UPred is typically the effective root of U, which has the functor PRED, but not necessarily. On the other hand, the elided predicate of NSU, called NSUPred, is the effective root of NSU and has the functor PRED. Fig. 3 describes U in more detail.

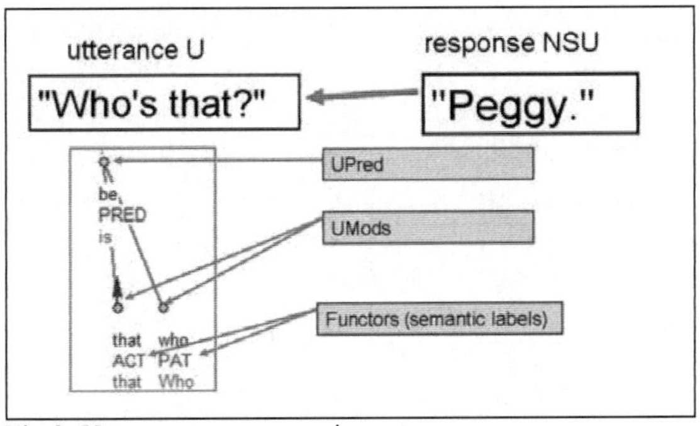

Fig 3. Utterance-response pair.

Whenever the clausal meaning of NSU can be reconstructed by using the copy of UPred as predicate, the t-lemma substitute for NSUPred is #VerbPron, which is normally also used for the pro-form do (dummy-do). NSUPred is always linked to UPred by a contextual-coreference arrow. When the clausal meaning of NSU cannot be directly reconstructed by using the copy of UPred as the predicate, NSUPred is rendered as the coreference-less t-lemma substitute #EmpVerb, which is normally used for cases of grammatical ellipsis of the predicate. #EmpVerb has no obligatory arguments and inherits no modifiers from anywhere. An NSUPred that has coreference inherits all modifiers from UPred, but these are not explicitly copied to NSUPred. NSUPred's own arguments are regarded as added to the inherited modifiers. Hence the NSU "Peggy." does not have to be explicitly reconstructed as "That is Peggy." (the left figure in Fig.4), but just with the coreferential predicate (the right figure).

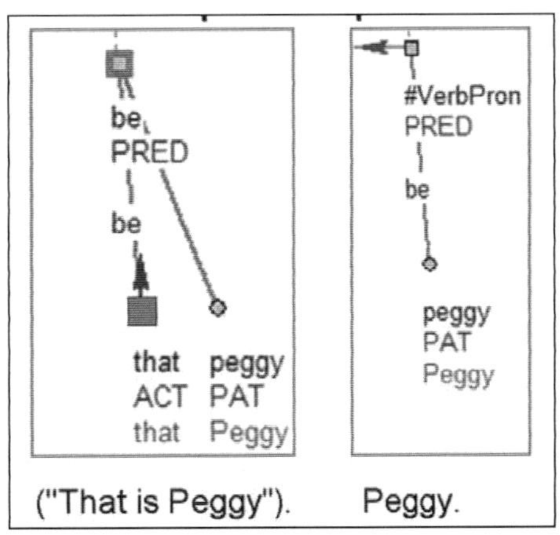

Fig. 4 Response NSU: Full explanative reconstruction (left) and the actual annotation resolution (right).

[2] NSU is regarded as a response even if U is a statement and NSU a question.

Obviously, NSUMods can be in a semantic conflict with the inherited UMods. These cases are marked by several types of arrows leading from the given NSUMod to the conflicting UMod in the antecedent utterance U. We distinguish four types of semantic conflict between NSUMod and UMod:

- overruling
- rephrasing
- wh-path
- other

3.6 Overruling

Overruling is the most typical semantic conflict where an NSUMod gives exactly the same type of information, but relating to a different entity in the real world. If NSU is to be expressed as a clause that uses the predicate of U, the conflicting UMod is erased (or prevented from inheriting) by the explicitly present NSUMod. E.g. in the following utterance-response pair:

U: I'm in a little place called Hellenthorpe.
NSU: Ellenthorpe.
NSU-paraphrase: *You are in a little place called ~~Hellenthorpe~~ Ellenthorpe.*

Even the explicit repetition is regarded as overruling:

U: There were just two people in the class.
NSU: Two people?.
NSU-paraphrase: *Were there just ~~two people~~ two people in the class?*

In the tree representation, the crossed text would be visible only in the tree of U, and an overruling-reference arrow would point at them from the relevant NSUMod. This conception prevents doubling the same modifier in NSU.

3.7 Rephrasing

When an NSUMod is rephrasing an UMod, then UMod and NSUMod refer to the same entity in the real world, or one refers to the entire entity whereas the other one refers only to its part, etc., using a different wording. The NSUMod-UMod relation marked as rephrasing is meant to become the starting material for bridging anaphora research. Example:

U: There were just two people in the class.
NSU: Just two students?
NSU-paraphrase: *Were there just ~~two people~~ two students in the class?*

It is also applied when the context is unambiguous for the speakers but ambiguous for the annotator, who lacks their background knowledge of the given situation. In the following example the annotator may not know whether `this part` or just the end of `this part` should come up, because he does not see the speakers pointing at the crane, but it is rather evident that it is not a completely different part of the crane but something at the end of it:

U1: You lift the crane, so this part comes up.
NSU1/U2: The end?
NSU1/U2-paraphrase1: Do you mean the end comes up?
NSU1/U2-paraphrase2: Do you mean the end of this part comes up?
NSU2/U3: Just this.
NSU3: Okay.

The category "Other" (see below) is though strongly preferred in ambiguous cases.

3.8 Wh-path[3]

The wh-path relation is the relation between the modifier that is focused by a wh-word in an U that is a direct or indirect question and a NSUMod that makes a good answer.

Overruling as well as rephrasing assume that the conflicting modifiers have the same functor. The wh-path category is different from the others in that it allows setting in conflict a UMod with an NSUMod with different semantic labels (functors). Our tentative annotation suggests that regular patterns will occur; e.g. with the question about direction/location. When asking `where`, speakers often get replies that would actually match questions `with whom` (functor ACMP) or `with which intention` (functor INTT,

[3] The term was found in Hajičová (1995) and reused by placing it in context with other response types.

e.g., `go shopping`), and yet they are perceived as good answers.

The relation between an utterance U which is a statement and an NSU which is a sluice is not wh-path but overruling. Cf.:

```
U: Where would you like to
go tomorrow?
NSU: Downtown with Mary, to
do some shopping.
```
(wh-path)

```
U: I would like to go down-
town with Mary tomorrow.
NSU: Where?
```
(overruling)

Sluices are not regarded as ambiguous in the sense whether referring to the same entity as the corresponding wh-word or not. They are not eligible for the relation "other" (see next section).

3.9 Other

"Other" is meant for inherently ambiguous cases of conflicting UMod and NSUMod where it is impossible to decide whether NSUMod is rephrasing or overruling UMod. Textual ambiguity arises when NSU is a question that does not find a proper answer in the context:

```
U1: He's got the best room.
NSU1/U2: Room 128?
NSU1/U2-paraphrase: Has he
got the best room Room 128?
U3: I don't know which num-
ber.
```

3.10 TR-Conditioned Criteria for NSU types

The original idea of the tectogrammatical representation of NSU was to adopt the taxonomy proposed by Fernández et al. (2007). However, the rules of TR made some classes collapse as they yielded identical tectogrammatical tree structures. The main criteria for tectogrammatical representation of NSU were the following:

Is the NSU a phrase or just an interjection? (Cf. Fig. 5 and 6)

- If it is a content word or a phrase, it should be reconstructed into a clause by adding a predicate.
- If it is an interjection except `yes` and `no` (and their colloquial variants), no predicate is added.
- If it is `yes/no` (and variants), a predicate should be added.
- If the interjection acts as a backchannel, `yes` and `no` make no exception.

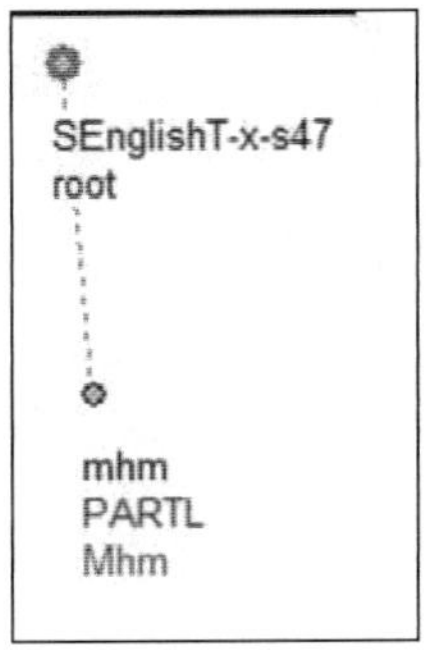

Fig. 5 Interjection

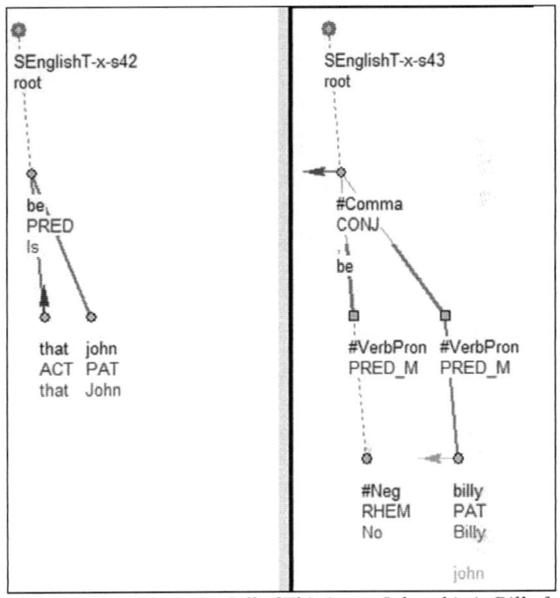

Fig. 6 *Is this John? No, Billy [This is not John, this is Billy.]*

Can we copy UPred to make NSU a clause?

- If we can, NSUPred has the t-lemma substitute `#VerbPron` and a coreferential arrow points from NSUPred to UPred.
- If we cannot, NSUPred has the t-lemma `#EmpVerb` with no coreferential arrow. No response type arrows point from NSUMods to UMods. In specific cases the coreference to UPred leads from elsewhere (Fig.7).

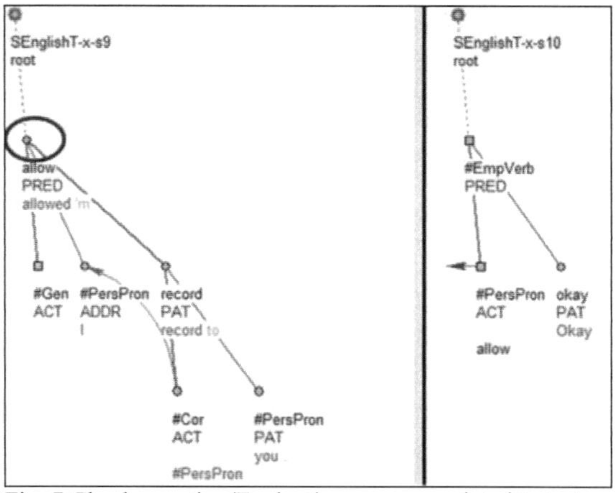

Fig. 7 Check question/Evaluative response related to text:

```
U: I am allowed to record you.
NSU (same speaker): Okay?
NSU-paraphrase: Is it (that I'm allowed
to record you) okay?
```

or

```
U: I am allowed to record you.
NSU (turn switch): Okay.
```

NSU-paraphrase: It <is> okay that you are allowed to record me.

3.11 More Examples of U-NSU relation resolution

Fernández et al. (2007) distinguish two types of sluice: the direct and the reprise sluice. In TR, each has a different semantic representation. The direct sluice has the coreferential predicate while the reprise sluice, which can be paraphrased as `What did you mean by saying this?`, has the empty-verb predicate and the wh-word gets the functor EFF, which is normally assigned to what is being said in the argument structure pattern of verbs of saying (Fig. 8).

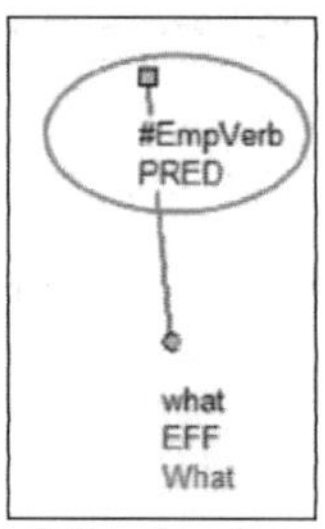

Fig. 8 Reprise sluice

Fig. 9 shows a sentence with wh-path linking modifiers with different functors.

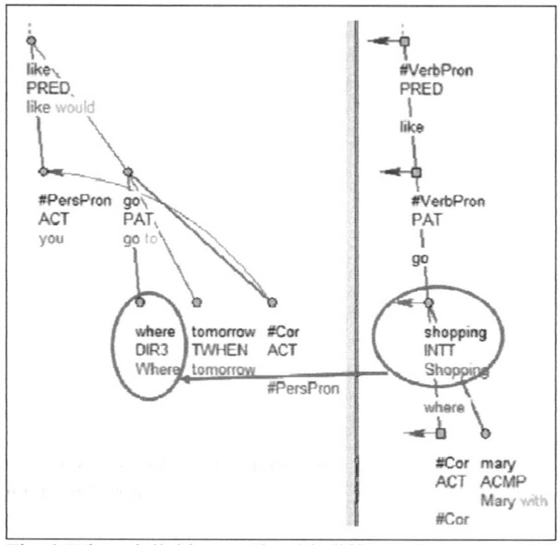

Fig. 9 Wh-path linking Mods with different functors

```
U: Where would you like to go tomorrow?
NSU: Shopping with Mary.
```

NSU-paraphrase: Tomorrow I would like to go shopping with Mary.

Choice questions (Fig.10) represent an interesting example in which one NSUMod can enter different relations to different UMods. The NSUMod `beer` overrules the coordinated UMod `Coke or Pepsi`, and at the same time it is connected with the wh-question `Which do you like to drink?` by wh-path.

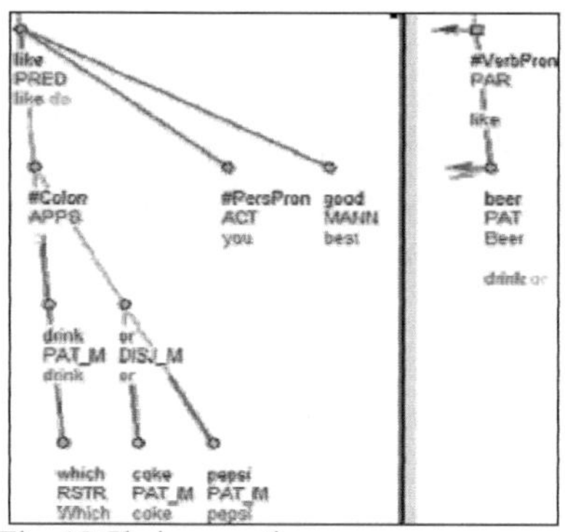

Fig. 10 Choice question.

```
U: Which do you like to drink: Coke or
Pepsi?
NSU: Beer.
```

NSU-paraphrase: I like to drink beer.

Seeing the many rephrasing cases in the data, which are supposed to be subject to further anaphora annotation (bridging etc.), we had to ask the question whether the boundary between response_type and coreference can be reliably determined. We found good evidence in the made-up but not unlikely example below (Fig.

11). In this context, `him` will be coreferential with `Paul` and `her` will be coreferential with `Mary`. On the other hand, `him` will overrule `Mary` and `her` will overrule `Paul` (only the relations of `him` are marked in the figure).

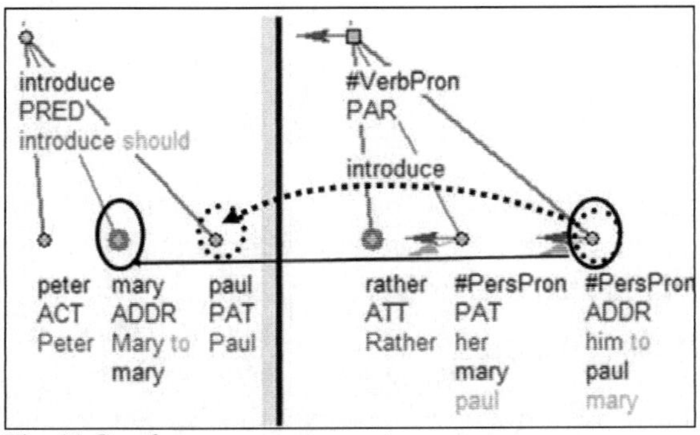

Fig. 11 Coreference vs. response type

3.12 Current and Future Work

The proposed enhancement of the annotation scheme has been tested on a corpus of approx. 200 NSUs with context manually extracted from the NAP transcripts as well as on example sentences from Fernández et al. (2007) and many sentences obtained by their modification performed in order to get potentially difficult counterexamples. As this is still a preparatory work, neither the inter-annotator agreement nor any other evaluation could be done so far.

In the next future, parts of the spoken corpora should get tectogrammatical parsing. The manual annotation is supposed to adopt this new feature of the annotation scheme, and we will try to incorporate it into our statistically trained automatic parsing tools.

Conclusion

The confrontation of our current annotation scheme with spoken dialog data has raised issues of ellipsis restoration and textual coreference in non-sentential utterances. We have found common relations between non-sentential utterances and their contexts, and we have integrated them into our semantic annotation scheme without violating its general principles. A tentative manual annotation of these relations in a small corpus suggests that such annotation is feasible. Further investigation on larger data along with machine-learning experiments is intended.

Acknowledgements

This work was funded in part by the Companions project (www.companions-project.org) sponsored by the European Commission as part of the Information Society Technologies (IST) programme under EC grant number IST-FP6-034434, as well as by the Czech Science Foundation (GA405/06/0589), and by the Czech Ministry of Education (MSM0021620838, MŠMT ČR LC536).

References

Jay Bradley, Oli Mival, and D. Benyon. 2008. A Novel Architecture for Designing by Wizard of Oz. In: Proceeding of CREATE08, British computer Society, Covent Garden, London, 24-25 June 2008.

Lou Burnard. 2000. Reference Guide for the British National Corpus (World Edition). Oxford University Computing Services. Available from ftp://sable.ox.ac.uk/pub/ota/BNC.

Silvie Cinková, Jan Hajič, Jan Ptáček. 2008. An Annotation Scheme for Speech Reconstruction on a Dialog Corpus. In Fourth International Workshop on Human-Computer Conversation. Bellagio, Italy: [http://www.companions-project.org/events/200810_bellagio.cfm],2008:1-6.

Raquel Fernández, Jonathan Ginzburg, and Shalom Lappin. 2007. Classifying Non-Sentential Utterances in Dialogue: A Machine Learning Approach. Computational Linguistics, Volume 33, Nr. 3. MIT Press for the Association for Computational Linguistics.

Erin Fitzgerald and Frederick Jelinek. 2008. Linguistic Resources for Reconstructing Spontaneous Speech Text. In: LREC 2008 Proceedings.

Jan Hajič, Silvie Cinková, Marie Mikulová, Petr Pajas, Jan Ptáček, Josef Toman, Zdeňka Urešová. 2008. PDTSL: An Annotated Resource For Speech Reconstruction. In Proceedings of the 2008 IEEE Workshop on Spoken Language Technology. IEEE, 2008.

Jan Hajič, Marie Mikulová, Martina Otradovcová, Petr Pajas, Nino Peterek, Pavel Češka, Miroslav Spousta. 2009. PDTSL - Prague Dependency Treebank of Spoken Language - Czech, Institute of Formal and Applied Linguistics, Charles University in Prague.

Eva Hajičová (ed.) 1995. Text And-Inference-Based Approach to Question Answering. Prague.

Petr Sgall, Eva Hajičová, and Jarmila Panevová. 1986. The Meaning of the Sentence in Its Semantic and Pragmatic Aspects. Dordrecht:Reidel Publishing Company and Prague:Academia.

Annotating Spoken Dialogs: from Speech Segments to Dialog Acts and Frame Semantics

Marco Dinarelli, Silvia Quarteroni, Sara Tonelli, Alessandro Moschitti, Giuseppe Riccardi*
University of Trento
38050 Povo - Trento, Italy
{dinarelli,silviaq,moschitti,riccardi}@disi.unitn.it, satonelli@fbk.eu

Abstract

We are interested in extracting semantic structures from spoken utterances generated within conversational systems. Current Spoken Language Understanding systems rely either on hand-written semantic grammars or on flat attribute-value sequence labeling. While the former approach is known to be limited in coverage and robustness, the latter lacks detailed relations amongst attribute-value pairs. In this paper, we describe and analyze the human annotation process of rich semantic structures in order to train semantic statistical parsers. We have annotated spoken conversations from both a human-machine and a human-human spoken dialog corpus. Given a sentence of the transcribed corpora, domain concepts and other linguistic features are annotated, ranging from e.g. part-of-speech tagging and constituent chunking, to more advanced annotations, such as syntactic, dialog act and predicate argument structure. In particular, the two latter annotation layers appear to be promising for the design of complex dialog systems. Statistics and mutual information estimates amongst such features are reported and compared across corpora.

1 Introduction

Spoken language understanding (SLU) addresses the problem of extracting and annotating the meaning structure from spoken utterances in the context of human dialogs (De Mori et al., 2008). In spoken dialog systems (SDS) most used models of SLU are based on the identification of slots (entities) within one or more frames (frame-slot semantics) that is defined by the application. While this model is simple and clearly insufficient to cope with interpretation and reasoning, it has supported the first generation of spoken dialog systems. Such dialog systems are thus limited by the ability to parse semantic features such as predicates and to perform logical computation in the context of a specific dialog act (Bechet et al., 2004). This limitation is reflected in the type of human-machine interactions which are mostly directed at querying the user for specific slots (e.g. "What is the departure city?") or implementing simple dialog acts (e.g. confirmation). We believe that an important step in overcoming such limitation relies on the study of models of human-human dialogs at different levels of representation: lexical, syntactic, semantic and discourse.

In this paper, we present our results in addressing the above issues in the context of the LUNA research project for next-generation spoken dialog interfaces (De Mori et al., 2008). We propose models for different levels of annotation of the LUNA spoken dialog corpus, including attribute-value, predicate argument structures and dialog acts. We describe the tools and the adaptation of off-the-shelf resources to carry out annotation of the predicate argument structures (PAS) of spoken utterances. We present a quantitative analysis of such semantic structures for both human-machine and human-human conversations.

To the best of our knowledge this is the first (human-machine and human-human) SDS corpus denoting a multilayer approach to the annotation of lexical, semantic and dialog features, which allows us to investigate statistical relations between the layers such as shallow semantic and discourse features used by humans or machines. In the following sections we describe the corpus, as well as a quantitative analysis and statistical correlations between annotation layers.

*This work was partially funded by the European Commission projects LUNA (contract 33549) and ADAMACH (contract 022593).

Proceedings of EACL 2009 Workshop on Semantic Representation of Spoken Language - SRSL 2009, pages 34–41,
Athens, Greece, 30 March 2009. ©2009 Association for Computational Linguistics

2 Annotation model

Our corpus is planned to contain 1000 equally partitioned Human-Human (HH) and Human-Machine (HM) dialogs. These are recorded by the customer care and technical support center of an Italian company. While HH dialogs refer to real conversations of users engaged in a problem solving task in the domain of software/hardware troubleshooting, HM dialogs are acquired with a Wizard of Oz approach (WOZ). The human agent (wizard) reacts to user's spontaneous spoken requests following one of ten possible dialog scenarios inspired by the services provided by the company.

The above data is organized in transcriptions and annotations of speech based on a new multi-level protocol studied specifically within the project, i.e. the annotation levels of words, turns[1], attribute-value pairs, dialog acts, predicate argument structures. The annotation at word level is made with part-of-speech and morphosyntactic information following the recommendations of EAGLES corpora annotation (Leech and Wilson, 2006). The attribute-value annotation uses a predefined domain ontology to specify concepts and their relations. Dialog acts are used to annotate intention in an utterance and can be useful to find relations between different utterances as the next section will show. For predicate structure annotation, we followed the FrameNet model (Baker et al., 1998) (see Section 2.2).

2.1 Dialog Act annotation

Dialog act annotation is the task of identifying the function or goal of a given utterance (Sinclair and Coulthard, 1975): thus, it provides a complementary information to the identification of domain concepts in the utterance, and a domain-independent dialog act scheme can be applied. For our corpus, we used a dialog act taxonomy which follows initiatives such as DAMSL (Core and Allen, 1997), TRAINS (Traum, 1996) and DIT++ (Bunt, 2005). Although the level of granularity and coverage varies across such taxonomies, a careful analysis leads to identifying three main groups of dialog acts:

1. *Core* acts, which represent the fundamental actions performed in the dialog, e.g. requesting and providing information, or executing a task. These include initiatives (often called forward-looking acts) and responses (backward-looking acts);
2. *Conventional/Discourse management* acts, which maintain dialog cohesion and delimit specific phases, such as opening, continuation, closing, and apologizing;
3. *Feedback/Grounding* acts,used to elicit and provide feedback in order to establish or restore a common ground in the conversation.

Our taxonomy, following the same three-fold partition, is summarized in Table 1.

Table 1: Dialog act taxonomy

Core dialog acts	
Info-request	Speaker wants information from addressee
Action-request	Speaker wants addressee to perform an action
Yes-answer	Affirmative answer
No-answer	Negative answer
Answer	Other kinds of answer
Offer	Speaker offers or commits to perform an action
ReportOnAction	Speaker notifies an action is being/has been performed
Inform	Speaker provides addressee with information not explicitly required (via an Info-request)
Conventional dialog acts	
Greet	Conversation opening
Quit	Conversation closing
Apology	Apology
Thank	Thanking (and down-playing)
Feedback/turn management dialog acts	
Clarif-request	Speaker asks addressee for confirmation/repetition of previous utterance for clarification.
Ack	Speaker expresses agreement with previous utterance, or provides feedback to signal understanding of what the addressee said
Filler	Utterance whose main goal is to manage conversational time (i.e. dpeaker taking time while keeping the turn)
Non-interpretable/non-classifiable dialog acts	
Other	Default tag for non-interpretable and non-classifiable utterances

It can be noted that we have decided to retain only the most frequent dialog act types from the schemes that inspired our work. Rather than aspiring to the full discriminative power of possible conversational situations, we have opted for a simple taxonomy that would cover the vast majority

[1] A turn is defined as the interval when a speaker is active, between two pauses in his/her speech flow.

of utterances and at the same time would be able to generalize them. Its small number of classes is meant to allow a supervised classification method to achieve reasonable performance with limited data. The taxonomy is currently used by the statistical Dialogue Manager in the ADAMACH EU project (Varges et al., 2008); the limited number of classes allows to reduce the number of hypothesized current dialogue acts, thus reducing the dialogue state space.

Dialog act annotation was performed manually by a linguist on speech transcriptions previously segmented into turns as mentioned above. The annotation unit for dialog acts, is the utterance; however, utterances are complex semantic entities that do not necessarily correspond to turns. Hence, a segmentation of the dialog transcription into utterances was performed by the annotator before dialog act labeling. Both utterance segmentation and dialog act labeling were performed through the MMAX tool (Müller and Strube, 2003).

The annotator proceeded according to the following guidelines:

1. by default, a turn is also an utterance;
2. if more than one tag is applicable to an utterance, choose the tag corresponding to its main function;
3. in case of doubt among several tags, give priority to tags in *core* dialog acts group;
4. when needed, split the turn into several utterances or merge several turns into one utterance.

Utterance segmentation provides the basis not only for dialog act labeling but also for the other semantic annotations. See Fig. 1 for a dialog sample where each line represents an utterance annotated according to the three levels.

2.2 Predicate Argument annotation

We carried out predicate argument structure annotation applying the FrameNet paradigm as described in (Baker et al., 1998). This model comprises a set of prototypical situations called *frames*, the frame-evoking words or expressions called *lexical units* and the roles or participants involved in these situations, called *frame elements*. The latter are typically the syntactic dependents of the lexical units. All lexical units belonging to the same frame have similar semantics and show

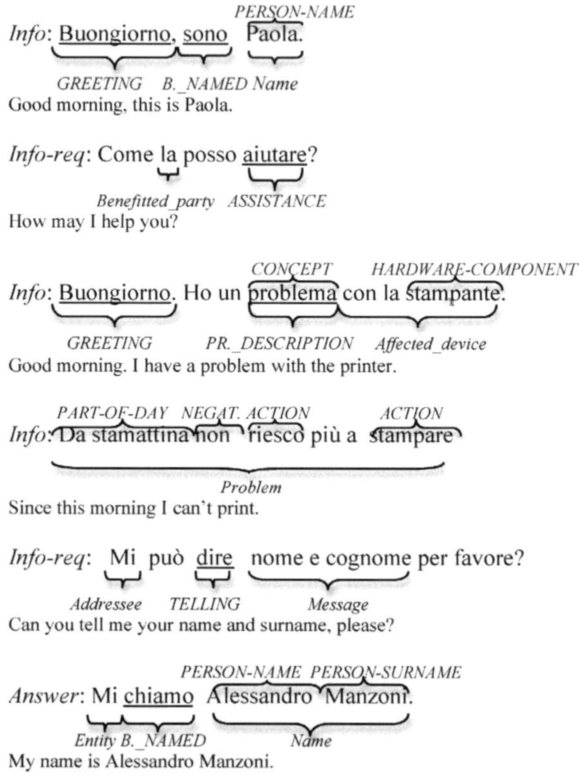

Figure 1: Annotated dialog extract. Each utterance is preceded by dialog act annotation. Attribute-value annotation appears above the text, PAS annotation below the text.

the same valence. A particular feature of the FrameNet project both for English and for other languages is its corpus-based nature, i.e. every element described in the resource has to be instantiated in a corpus. To annotate our SDS corpus, we adopted where possible the already existing frame and frame element descriptions defined for the English FrameNet project, and introduced new definitions only in case of missing elements in the original model.

Figure 1 shows a dialog sample with PAS annotation reported below the utterance. All lexical units are underlined and the frame is written in capitals, while the other labels refer to frame elements. In particular, *ASSISTANCE* is evoked by the lexical unit *aiutare* and has one attested frame element (*Benefitted_party*), *GREETING* has no frame element, and *PROBLEM_DESCRIPTION* and *TELLING* have two frame elements each.

Figure 2 gives a comprehensive view of the annotation process, from audio file transcription to the annotation of three semantic layers. Whereas

Figure 2: The annotation process

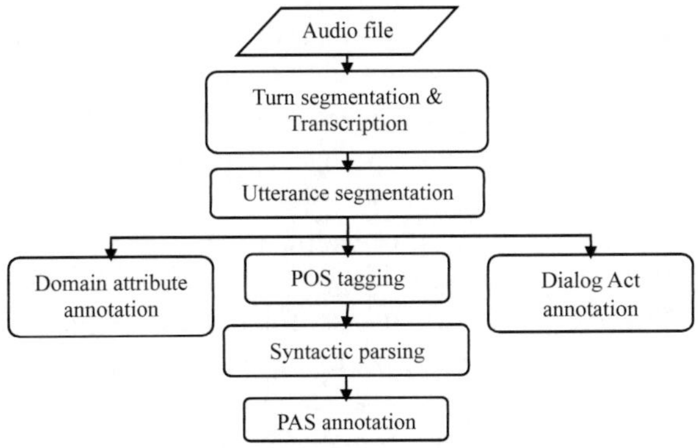

attribute-value and DA annotation are carried out on the segmented dialogs at utterance level, PAS annotation requires POS-tagging and syntactic parsing (via Bikel's parser trained for Italian (Corazza et al., 2007)). Finally, a shallow manual correction is carried out to make sure that the tree nodes that may carry semantic information have correct constituent boundaries. For the annotation of frame information, we used the *Salto* tool (Burchardt et al., 2006), that stores the dialog file in TIGER-XML format and allows to easily introduce word tags and frame flags. Frame information is recorded on top of parse trees, with target information pointing to terminal words and frame elements pointing to tree nodes.

3 Quantitative comparison of the Annotation

We evaluated the outcome of dialog act and PAS annotation levels on both the human-human (henceforth HH) and human-machine (HM) corpora by not only analyzing frequencies and occurrences in the separate levels, but also their interaction, as discussed in the following sections.

3.1 Dialog Act annotation

Analyzing the annotation of 50 HM and 50 HH dialogs at the dialog act level, we note that an HH dialog is composed in average by 48.9 ± 17.4 (standard deviation) dialog acts, whereas a HM dialog is composed of 18.9 ± 4.4. The difference between average lengths shows how HH spontaneous speech can be redundant, while HM dialogs are more limited to an exchange of essential information. The standard deviation of a conversation in terms of dialog acts is considerably higher in the HH corpus than in the HM one. This can be explained by the fact that the WOZ follows a unique, previously defined task-solving strategy that does not allow for digressions. Utterance segmentation was also performed differently on the two corpora. In HH we performed 167 turn mergings and 225 turn splittings; in HM dialogs, only turn splittings (158) but no turn mergings were performed.

Tables 2 and 3 report the dialog acts occurring in the HM and HH corpora, respectively, ranked by their frequencies.

Table 2: Dialog acts ranked by frequency in the human-machine (HM) corpus

human-machine (HM)		
DA	count	rel. freq.
Info-request	249	26.3%
Answer	171	18.1%
Inform	163	17.2%
Yes-answer	70	7.4%
Quit	60	6.3%
Thank	56	5.9%
Greet	50	5.3%
Offer	49	5.2%
Clarification-request	26	2.7%
Action-request	25	2.6%
Ack	12	1.3%
Filler	6	0.6%
No-answer	5	0.5%
Other, ReportOnAction	2	0.2%
Apology	1	0.1%
TOTAL	947	

From a comparative analysis, we note that:

1. *info-request* is by far the most common dialog act in HM, whereas in HH *ack* and *info* share the top ranking position;
2. the most frequently occurring dialog act in HH, i.e. *ack*, is only ranked 11th in HM;
3. the relative frequency of *clarification-request* (4,7%) is considerably higher in HH than in HM.

We also analyzed the ranking of the most frequent dialog act bigrams in the two corpora. We can summarize our comparative analysis, reported in Table 4, to the following: in both corpora, most bigram types contain *info* and *info-request*,

Table 3: Dialog acts ranked by frequency in the human-human (HH) corpus

human-human (HH)		
DA	count	rel. freq.
Ack	582	23.8%
Inform	562	23.0%
Info-request	303	12.4%
Answer	192	7.8%
Clarification-request	116	4.7%
Offer	114	4.7%
Yes-answer	112	4.6%
Quit	101	4.1%
ReportOnAction	91	3.7%
Other	70	2.9%
Action-request	69	2.8%
Filler	61	2.5%
Thank	33	1.3%
No-answer	26	1.1%
Greet, Apology	7	0.3%
TOTAL	2446	

as expected in a troubleshooting system. However, the bigram *info-request answer*, which we expected to form the core of a task-solving dialog, is only ranked 5th in the HH corpus, while 5 out of the top 10 bigram types contain *ack*. We believe that this is because HH dialogs primarily contain spontaneous information-providing turns (e.g. several *info info* by the same speaker) and acknowledgements for the purpose of backchannel. Instead, HM dialogs, structured as sequences of *info-request answers* pairs, are more minimal and brittle, showing how users tend to avoid redundancy when addressing a machine.

Table 4: The 10 most frequent dialog act bigrams

human-machine (HM)	human-human (HH)
info-req answer	ack info
answer info-req	info ack
info info-req	info info
info-req y-answer	ack ack
sentence_beginning greet	info-req answer
greet info	info info-req
info quit	info-req y-answer
offer info	ack info-req
thank info	answer ack
y-answer thank	quit *sentence_end*

3.2 Predicate Argument annotation

We annotated 50 HM and 50 HH dialogs with frame information. Differently from the English FrameNet database, we didn't annotate one frame per sentence. On the contrary, we identified all lexical units corresponding to "semantically relevant" verbs, nouns and adjectives with a syntactic subcategorization pattern, eventually skipping the utterances with empty semantics (e.g. disfluencies). In particular, we annotated all lexical units that imply an action, introduce the speaker's opinion or describe the office environment. We introduced 20 new frames out of the 174 identified in the corpus because the original definition of frames related to hardware/software, data-handling and customer assistance was sometimes too coarse-grained. Few new frame elements were introduced as well, mostly expressing syntactic realizations that are typical of spoken Italian.

Table 5 shows some statistics about the corpus dimension and the results of our annotation. The human-human dialogs contain less frame instances in average than the human-machine group, meaning that speech disfluencies, not present in turns uttered by the WOZ, negatively affect the semantic density of a turn. For the same reason, the percentage of turns in HH dialogs that were manually corrected in the pre-processing step (see Section 2.2) is lower than for HM turns, since HH dialogs have more turns that are semantically empty and that were skipped in the correction phase. Besides, HH dialogs show a higher frame variability than HM, which can be explained by the fact that spontaneous conversation may concern minor topics, whereas HM dialogs follow a previously defined structure, designed to solve software/hardware problems.

Tables 6 and 7 report the 10 most frequent frames occurring in the human-machine resp. human-human dialogs. The relative frame frequency in HH dialogs is more sparse than in HM dialogs, meaning that the task-solving strategy followed by the WOZ limits the number of digressions, whereas the semantics of HH dialogs is richer and more variable.

As mentioned above, we had to introduce and define new frames which were not present in the original FrameNet database for English in order to capture all relevant situations described in the dialogs. A number of these frames appear in both tables, suggesting that the latter are indeed rel-

Table 5: Dialog turn and frame statistics for the human-machine (HM) resp. human-human (HH) corpus

	HM	HH
Total number of turns	662	1,997
Mean dialog length (turns)	13.2	39.9
Mean turn length (tokens)	11.4	10.8
Corrected turns (%)	50	39
Total number of annotations	923	1951
Mean number of frame annotations per dialog	18.5	39.0
Mean number of frame elements per frame annotation	1.6	1.7

Table 6: The 10 most frequent frames in the HM corpus (* =newly introduced)

HM corpus		
Frame	count	freq-%
Greeting*	146	15.8
Telling	134	14.5
Recording	83	8.9
Being_named	74	8.0
Contacting	52	5.6
Usefulness	50	5.4
Being_operational	28	3.0
Problem_description*	24	2.6
Inspecting	24	2.6
Perception_experience	21	2.3

Table 7: The 10 most frequent frames in the HH corpus (* =newly introduced)

HH corpus		
Frame	count	freq-%
Telling	143	7.3
Greeting*	124	6.3
Awareness	74	3.8
Contacting	63	3.2
Giving	62	3.2
Navigation*	61	3.1
Change_operational_state	51	2.6
Perception_experience	46	2.3
Insert_data*	46	2.3
Come_to_sight*	38	1.9

evant to model the general semantics of the dialogs we are approaching. The most frequent frame group comprises frames relating to information exchange that is typical of the help-desk activity, including *Telling*, *Greeting*, *Contacting*, *Statement*, *Recording*, *Communication*. Another relevant group encompasses frames related to the operational state of a device, for example *Being_operational*, *Change_operational_state*, *Operational_testing*, *Being_in_operation*.

The two groups also show high variability of lexical units. *Telling*, *Change_operational_state* and *Greeting* have the richest lexical unit set, with 11 verbs/nouns/adjectives each. *Arriving* and *Awareness* are expressed by 10 different lexical units, while *Statement*, *Being_operational*, *Removing* and *Undergo_change_of_operational_state* have 9 different lexical units each. The informal nature of the spoken dialogs influences the composition of the lexical unit sets. In fact, they are rich in verbs and multiwords used only in colloquial contexts, for which there are generally few attestations in the English FrameNet database.

Similarly to the dialog act statistics, we also analyzed the most frequent frame bigrams and trigrams in HM and HH dialogs. Results are reported in Tables 8 and 9. Both HH bigrams and trigrams show a more sparse distribution and lower relative frequency than HM ones, implying that HH dialogs follow a more flexible structure with a richer set of topics, thus the sequence of themes is less predictable. In particular, 79% of HH bigrams and 97% of HH trigrams occur only once (vs. 68% HM bigrams and 82% HM trigrams). On the contrary, HM dialogs deal with a fix sequence of topics driven by the turns uttered by the WOZ. For instance, the most frequent HM bigram and trigram both correspond to the opening utterance of the WOZ:

*Help desk buongiorno*GREETING, *sono*BEING_NAMED *Paola, in cosa posso esserti utile*USEFULNESS*?*
(Good morning, help-desk service, Paola speaking, how can I help you?)

3.3 Mutual information between PAS and dialog acts

A unique feature of our corpus is the availability of both a semantic and a dialog act annotation level: it is intuitive to seek relationships in the purpose of improving the recognition and understanding of each level by using features from the other. We considered a subset of 20 HH and 50 HM dialogs and computed an initial analysis

Table 8: The 5 most frequent frame bigrams

human-machine (HM)	freq-%
Greeting Being_named	17.1
Being_named Usefulness	15.3
Telling Recording	12.9
Recording Contacting	10.9
Contacting Greeting	10.6
human-human (HH)	**freq-%**
Greeting Greeting	4.7
Navigation Navigation	1.2
Telling Telling	1.0
Change_op._state Change_op._state	0.9
Telling Problem_description	0.8

Table 9: The 5 most frequent frame trigrams

human-machine (HM)	freq-%
Greeting Being_named Usefulness	9.5
Recording Contacting Greeting	5.7
Being_named Usefulness Greeting	3.7
Telling Recording Contacting	3.5
Telling Recording Recording	2.2
human-human (HH)	**freq-%**
Greeting Greeting Greeting	1.6
Greeting Being_named Greeting	0.5
Contacting Greeting Greeting	0.3
Navigation Navigation Navigation	0.2
Working_on Greeting Greeting	0.2

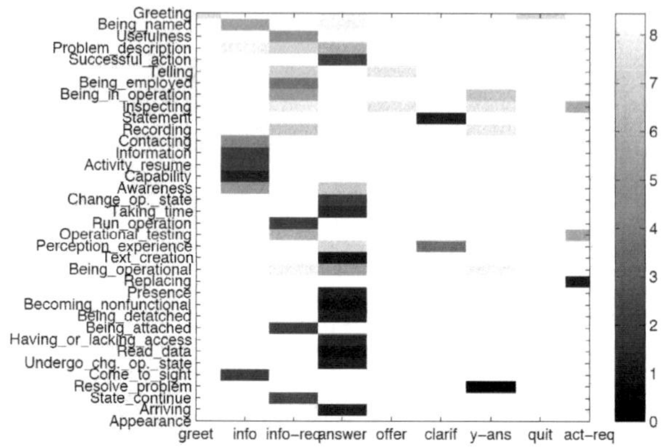

(a) human-machine dialogs (filtering co-occurrences below 3)

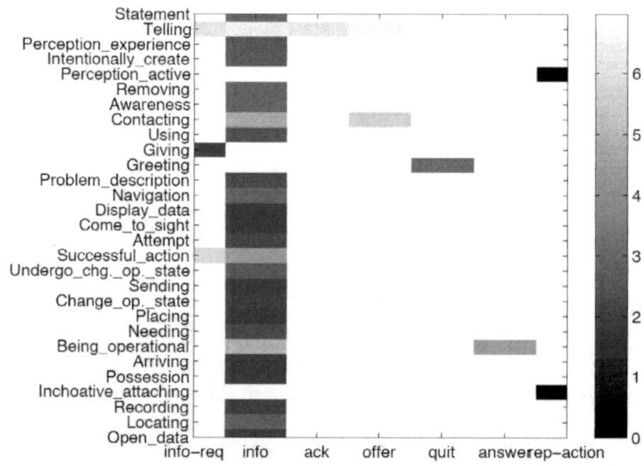

(b) human-human dialogs (filtering co-occurrences below 5)

Figure 3: Weighted conditional entropy between PAS and dialog acts in the HM (a) and HH corpus (b). To lower entropies correspond higher values of mutual information (darker color in the scale)

of the co-occurrences of dialog acts and PAS. We noted that each PAS tended to co-occur only with a limited subset of the available dialog act tags, and moreover in most cases the co-occurrence happened with only one dialog act. For a more thorough analysis, we computed the weighted conditional entropy between PAS and dialog acts, which yields a direct estimate of the mutual information between the two levels of annotation[2].

Our results are illustrated in Figure 3. In the HM corpus (Fig. 3(a)), we noted some interesting associations between dialog acts and PAS. First, `info-req` has the maximal MI with PAS like *Being_in_operation* and *Being_attached*, as requests are typically used by the operator to get information about the status of device. Several PAS denote a high MI with the `info` dialog act, including *Activity_resume, Information, Being_named, Contacting*, and *Resolve_problem*. *Contacting* refers to the description of the situation and of the speaker's point of view (usually the caller). *Being_named* is primarily employed when the caller introduces himself, while *Activity_resume* usually refers to the operator's description of the sched-

[2] Let $H(y_j|x_i)$ be the weighted conditional entropy of observation y_j of variable Y given observation x_i of variable X:

$$H(y_j|x_i) = -p(x_i; y_j) log \frac{p(x_i; y_j)}{p(x_i)},$$

where $p(x_i; y_j)$ is the probability of co-occurrence of x_i and y_j, and $p(x_i)$ and $p(y_j)$ are the marginal probabilities of occurrence of x_i resp. y_j in the corpus. There is an obvious relation with the weighted mutual information between x_i and y_j, defined following e.g. (Bechet et al., 2004) as:

$$wMI(x_i; y_j) = p(x_i; y_j) log \frac{p(x_i; y_j)}{p(x_i)p(y_j)}.$$

Indeed, the higher is $H(y_j|x_i)$, the lower is $wMI(x_i; y_j)$. We approximate all probabilities using frequency of occurrence.

uled interventions.

As for the remaining acts, `clarif` has the highest MI with *Perception_experience* and *Statement*, used to warn the addressee about understanding problems and asking him to repeat/rephrase an utterance, respectively. The two strategies can be combined in the same utterance, as in the utterance: *Non ho sentito bene: per favore ripeti cercando di parlare più forte.* (I haven't quite heard that, please repeat trying to speak up.).

The `answer` tag is highly informative with *Successful_action, Change_operational_state, Becoming_nonfunctional, Being_detached, Read_data*. These PAS refer to the exchange of information (*Read_data*) or to actions performed by the user after a suggestion of the system (*Change_operational_state*). Action requests (act-req) seem to be correlated to *Replacing* as it usually occurs when the operator requests the caller to carry out an action to solve a problem, typically to replace a component with another. Another frequent request may refer to some device that the operator has to test.

In the HH corpus (Fig. 3(b)), most of the PAS are highly mutually informative with `info`: indeed, as shown in Table 3, this is the most frequently occurring act in HH except for `ack`, which rarely contain verbs that can be annotated by a frame. As for the remaining acts, there is an easily explainable high MI between `quit` and *Greeting*; moreover, `info-req` denote its highest MI with *Giving*, as in requests to give information, while `rep-action` denotes a strong co-occurrence with *Inchoative_attaching*: indeed, interlocutors often report on the action of connecting a device.

These results corroborate our initial observation that for most PAS, the mutual information tends to be very high in correspondence of one dialog act type: this suggests the beneficial effect of including shallow semantic information as features for dialog act classification. The converse is less clear as the same dialog act can relate to a span of words covered by multiple PAS and generally, several PAS co-occur with the same dialog act.

4 Conclusions

In this paper we have proposed an approach to the annotation of spoken dialogs using semantic and discourse features. Such effort is crucial to investigate the complex dependencies between the layers of semantic processing. We have designed the annotation model to incorporate features and models developed both in the speech and language research community and bridging the gap between the two communities. Our multi-layer annotation corpus allows the investigation of cross-layer dependencies and across human-machine and human-human dialogs as well as training of semantic models which accounts for predicate interpretation.

References

C. F. Baker, C. J. Fillmore, and J. B. Lowe. 1998. The Berkeley FrameNet Project. In *Proceedings of ACL/Coling'98*, pages 86–90.

F. Bechet, G. Riccardi, and D. Hakkani-Tur. 2004. Mining spoken dialogue corpora for system evaluation and modeling. In *Proceedings of EMNLP'04*, pages 134–141.

H. Bunt. 2005. A framework for dialogue act specication. In *Proceedings of SIGSEM WG on Representation of Multimodal Semantic Information*.

A. Burchardt, K. Erk, A. Frank, A. Kowalski, S. Padó, and M. Pinkal. 2006. Salto - a versatile multi-level annotation tool. In *Proceedings of LREC 2006*, pages 517–520, Genoa, Italy.

A. Corazza, A. Lavelli, and G. Satta. 2007. Analisi sintattica-statistica basata su costituenti. *Intelligenza Artificiale*, 4(2):38–39.

M. G. Core and J. F. Allen. 1997. Coding dialogs with the DAMSL annotation scheme. In *Proceedings of the AAAI Fall Symposium on Communicative Actions in Humans and Machines*.

R. De Mori, F. Bechet, D. Hakkani-Tur, M. McTear, G. Riccardi, and G. Tur. 2008. Spoken language understanding: A survey. *IEEE Signal Processing magazine*, 25(3):50–58.

G. Leech and A. Wilson. 2006. EAGLES recommendations for the morphosyntactic annotation of corpora. Technical report, ILC-CNR.

C. Müller and M. Strube. 2003. Multi-level annotation in MMAX. In *Proceedings of SIGDIAL'03*.

J. M. Sinclair and R. M. Coulthard. 1975. *Towards an Analysis of Discourse: The English Used by Teachers and Pupils*. Oxford University Press, Oxford.

D. Traum. 1996. Conversational agency: The TRAINS-93 dialogue manager. In *Proceedings of TWLT 11: Dialogue Management in Natural Language Systems*, pages 1–11, June.

S. Varges, G. Riccardi, and S. Quarteroni. 2008. Persistent information state in a data-centric architecture. In *Proceedings of SIGDIAL'08*.

Predicting Concept Types in User Corrections in Dialog

Svetlana Stoyanchev and **Amanda Stent**
Department of Computer Science
Stony Brook University
Stony Brook, NY 11794-4400, USA
svetlana.stoyanchev@gmail.com, amanda.stent@stonybrook.edu

Abstract

Most dialog systems explicitly confirm user-provided task-relevant concepts. User responses to these system confirmations (e.g. corrections, topic changes) may be misrecognized because they contain unrequested task-related concepts. In this paper, we propose a *concept-specific language model adaptation strategy* where the language model (LM) is adapted to the concept type(s) actually present in the user's post-confirmation utterance. We evaluate concept type classification and LM adaptation for post-confirmation utterances in the *Let's Go!* dialog system. We achieve 93% accuracy on concept type classification using acoustic, lexical and dialog history features. We also show that the use of concept type classification for LM adaptation can lead to improvements in speech recognition performance.

1 Introduction

In most dialog systems, the system explicitly confirms user-provided task-relevant *concepts*. The user's response to a confirmation prompt such as "leaving from Waterfront?" may consist of a simple *confirmation* (e.g. "yes"), a simple *rejection* (e.g. "no"), a *correction* (e.g. "no, Oakland") or a *topic change* (e.g. "no, leave at 7" or "yes, and go to Oakland"). Each type of utterance has implications for further processing. In particular, corrections and topic changes are likely to contain unrequested task-relevant concepts that are not well represented in the recognizer's post-confirmation language model (LM)[1]. This means that they are likely to be misrecognized, frustrating the user and leading to cascading errors. Correct determination of the content of post-confirmation utterances can lead to improved speech recognition, fewer and shorter sequences of speech recognition errors, and improved dialog system performance.

In this paper, we look at user responses to system confirmation prompts CMU's deployed *Let's Go!* dialog system. We adopt a two-pass recognition architecture (Young, 1994). In the first pass, the input utterance is processed using a general-purpose LM (e.g. specific to the domain, or specific to the dialog state). Recognition may fail on concept words such as "Oakland" or "61C" , but is likely to succeed on closed-class words (e.g. "yes", "no", "and", "but", "leaving"). If the utterance follows a system confirmation prompt, we then use acoustic, lexical and dialog history features to determine the task-related *concept type(s)* likely to be present in the utterance. In the second recognition pass, any utterance containing a concept type is re-processed using a concept-specific LM. We show that: (1) it is possible to achieve high accuracy in determining presence or absence of particular concept types in a post-confirmation utterance; and (2) 2-pass speech recognition with concept type classification and language model adaptation can lead to improved speech recognition performance for post-confirmation utterances.

The rest of this paper is structured as follows: In Section 2 we discuss related work. In Section 3 we describe our data. In Section 4 we present our concept type classification experiment. In Section 5 we present our LM adaptation experiment. In Section 6 we conclude and discuss future work.

[1] The word error rate on post-confirmation *Let's Go!* utterances containing a concept is 10% higher than on utterances without a concept.

Proceedings of EACL 2009 Workshop on Semantic Representation of Spoken Language - SRSL 2009, pages 42–49,
Athens, Greece, 30 March 2009.

2 Related Work

When a dialog system requests a confirmation, the user's subsequent corrections and topic change utterances are particularly likely to be misrecognized. Considerable research has now been done on the automatic detection of spoken corrections. Linguistic cues to corrections include the number of words in the post-confirmation utterance and the use of marked word order (Krahmer et al., 2001). Prosodic cues include F0 max, RMS max, RMS mean, duration, speech tempo, and percentage of silent frames(Litman et al., 2006; Hirschberg et al., 2004; Levow, 1998). Discourse cues include the removal, repetition, addition or modification of a concept, the system's dialog act type, and information about error rates in the dialog so far (Krahmer et al., 2001; et al., 2002; Litman et al., 2006; Walker et al., 2000). In our experiments, we use most of these features as well as additional lexical features.

We can use knowledge of the type or content of a user utterance to modify system behavior. For example, in this paper we use the concept type(s) in the user's utterance to adapt the recognizer's LM. It is now common practice to adapt the recognizer to the type, context or style of input speech (Bellegarda, 2004). LM adaptation has been used to improve automatic speech recognition performance in automated meeting transcription (Tur and Stolcke, 2007), speech-driven question answering (Stenchikova et al., 2008), broadcast news recognition (Gildea and Hofmann, 1999), and spoken dialog systems (Tur, 2005). LMs in dialog systems can be adapted to the dialog state (e.g. (Riccardi and Gorin, 2000; Esteve et al., 2001)), the topic (Iyer and Ostendorf, 1999; Gildea and Hofmann, 1999), or the speaker (Tur, 2007).

3 Data

In this experiment we use annotated dialog transcripts and speech from the *Let's Go!* system, a telephone-based spoken dialog system that provides information about bus routes in Pittsburgh (Raux et al., 2005). The data we used comes from the first two months of *Let's Go!* system operation in 2005 (2411 dialogs), and one month in 2006 (1430 dialogs). This data has been transcribed, and annotated by hand for concept types.

In order to provide the user with route information, *Let's Go!* must elicit a departure location, a destination, a departure time, and optionally a bus route number. Each concept value provided by the user is explicitly confirmed by the system (see Figure 1). In the annotated transcripts, the following *concepts* are labeled: `neighborhood`, `place`, `time`, `hour`, `minute`, `time-of-day`, and `bus`. For our experiments we collapsed these concepts into three *concept types*: *time* , *place* and *bus*.

1	Sys	Welcome to the CMU Let's Go bus information system. What can I do for you?
2	User	I need to go from Oakland**:p**
	ASR	*I need to go .from. can't*
3	Sys	Where do you wanna leave from?
4	User	to Waterfront**:p**
	ASR	*told. .me. Waterfront*
5	Sys	Leaving from WATERFRONT . Did I get that right?
6	User	OAKLAND**:p**
	ASR	*OAKLAND*
7	Sys	Leaving from OAKLAND . Did I get that right?

Figure 1: Dialog extract from *Let's Go!* data. User utterances are annotated with concept types (e.g. :p for place)

Let's Go! has five dialog states corresponding to the type of user utterance it expects: *first-query*, *next-query*, *yes-no*, *place* and *time*. Its speech recognizer uses dialog state-specific n-gram LMs trained on user utterances from the 2005 data. We focus on user utterances in response to system confirmation prompts (the *yes-no* state). Table 1 shows statistics about *yes-no* state utterances in *Let's Go!*. Table 2 shows a confusion matrix for confirmation prompt concept type and post-confirmation utterance concept type. This table indicates the potential for misrecognition of post-confirmation utterances. For example, in the 2006 dataset after a system confirmation prompt for a *bus*, a *bus* concept is used in only 64% of concept-containing user utterances.

In our experiments, we used the 2006 data to train concept type classifiers and for testing. We used the 2005 data to build LMs for our speech recognition experiment.

4 Concept Classification

4.1 Method

Our goal is to classify each post-confirmation user utterance by the concept type(s) it contains (*place, time, bus* or *none*) for later language-model adaptation (see Section 5). From the post-confirmation user utterances in the 2006 dataset described in

Event	2005		2006	
	num	%	num	%
Total dialogs	2411		1430	
Total yes-no confirms	9098	100	9028	100
Yes-no confirms with a concept	2194	24	1635	18.1
Dialog State				
Total confirm place utts	5548	61	5347	59.2
Total confirm bus utts	1763	19.4	1589	17.6
Total confirm time utts	1787	19.6	2011	22.3
Concept Type Features				
Yes-no utts with place	1416	15.6	1007	11.2
Yes-no utts with time	296	3.2	305	3.4
Yes-no utts with bus	584	6.4	323	3.6
Lexical Features				
Yes-no utts with 'yes'	4395	48.3	3693	40.9
Yes-no utts with 'no'	2076	22.8	1564	17.3
Yes-no utts with 'I'	203	2.2	129	1.4
Yes-no utts with 'from'	114	1.3	185	2.1
Yes-no utts with 'to'	204	2.2	237	2.6
Acoustic Features				
feature	mean	stdev	mean	stdev
Duration (seconds)	1.341	1.097	1.365	1.242
RMS mean	.037	.033	.055	.049
F0 mean	183.0	60.86	185.7	58.63
F0 max	289.8	148.5	296.9	146.5

Table 1: Statistics on post-confirmation utterances

	place	bus	time
2005 dataset			
confirm_place	0.86	0.13	0.01
confirm_bus	0.18	0.81	0.01
confirm_time	0.07	0.01	0.92
2006 dataset			
confirm_place	0.87	0.10	0.03
confirm_bus	0.34	0.64	0.02
confirm_time	0.15	0.13	0.71

Table 2: Confirmation state vs. user concept type

Section 3, we extracted the features described in Section 4.2 below. To identify the correct concept type(s) for each utterance, we used the human annotations provided with the data.

We performed a series of 10-fold cross-validation experiments to examine the impact of different types of feature on concept type classification. We trained three binary classifiers for each experiment, one for each concept type, i.e. we separately classified each post-confirmation utterance as *place* + or *place* -, *time* + or *time* -, and *bus* + or *bus* -. We used Weka's implementation of the J48 decision tree classifier (Witten and Frank, 2005)[2].

For each experiment, we report precision (*pre*+) and recall (*rec*+) for determining *presence* of each concept type, and overall classification accuracy for each concept type (*place, bus* and *time*)[3]. We also report overall *pre*+, *rec*+, f-measure (*f*+), and classification accuracy across the three concept types. Finally, we report the percentage of *switch*+ errors and *switch* errors. *Switch*+ errors are utterances containing *bus* classified as *time/place*, *time* as *bus/place*, and *place* as *bus/time*; these are the errors most likely to cause decreases in speech recognition accuracy after language model adaptation. *Switch* errors include utterances with no concept classified as *place*, *bus* or *time*.

Only utterances classified as containing one of the three concept types are subject to second-pass recognition using a concept-specific language model. Therefore, these are the only utterances on which speech recognition performance may improve. This means that we want to maximize *rec*+ (proportion of utterances containing a concept that are classified correctly). On the other hand, utterances that are incorrectly classified as containing a particular concept type will be subject to second-pass recognition using a poorly-chosen language model. This may cause speech recognition performance to suffer. This means that we want to minimize *switch*+ errors.

4.2 Features

We used the features summarized in Table 3. All of these features are available at run-time and so may be used in a live system. Below we give additional information about the RAW and LEX features; the other feature sets are self-explanatory.

4.2.1 Acoustic and Dialog History Features

The acoustic/prosodic and dialog history features are adapted from those identified in previous work on detecting speech recognition errors (particularly (Litman et al., 2006)). We anticipated that these features would help us distinguish corrections and rejections from confirmations.

4.2.2 Lexical Features

We used lexical features from the user's current utterance. Words in the output of first-pass ASR are highly indicative both of concept presence or absence, and of the presence of particular concept types; for example, *going to* suggests the presence of a *place*. We selected the most salient lexi-

[2] J48 gave the highest classification accuracy compared to other machine learning algorithms we tried on this data.

[3] We do not report precision or recall for determining *absence* of each concept type. In our data set 82.2% of the utterances do not contain any concepts (see Table 1). Consequently, precision and recall for determining absence of each concept type are above .9 in each of the experiments.

Feature type	Feature source	Features
System confirmation type (DIA)	system log	System's confirmation prompt concept type (*confirm_time, confirm_place, or confirm_bus*)
Acoustic (RAW)	raw speech	F0 max; RMS max; RMS mean; Duration; Difference between F0 max in first half and in second half
Lexical (LEX)	transcripts/ASR output	Presence of specific lexical items; Number of tokens in utterance; [transcribed speech only] String edit distance between current and previous user utterances
Dialog history (DH1, DH3)	1-3 previous utterances	System's dialog states of previous utterances(*place, bus, time, confirm_time, confirm_place, or confirm_bus*); [transcribed speech only] Concept(s) that occurred in user's utterances (YES/NO for each of the concepts *place, bus, time*)
ASR confidence score (ASR)	ASR output	Speech recognizer confidence score
Concept type match (CTM)	transcripts/ASR output	Presence of concept-specific lexical items

Table 3: Features for concept type classifiers

cal features (unigrams and bigrams) for each concept type by computing the *mutual information* between potential features and concept types (Manning et al., 2008). For each lexical feature t and each concept type class $c \in \{$ *place +, place -, time +, time -, bus +, bus -*$\}$, we computed *I*:

$$I = \frac{N_{tc}}{N} * log_2 \frac{N * N_{tc}}{N_{t.} * N_{.c}} + \frac{N_{0c}}{N} * log_2 \frac{N * N_{0c}}{N_{0.} * N_{.c}} + \frac{N_{t0}}{N} * log_2 \frac{N * N_{t0}}{N_{t.} * N_{.0}} + \frac{N_{00}}{N} * log_2 \frac{N * N_{00}}{N_{0.} * N_{.0}}$$

where N_{tc}= number of utterances where t co-occurs with c, N_{0c}= number of utterances with c but without t, N_{t0}= number of utterances where t occurs without c, N_{00}= number of utterances with neither t nor c, $N_{t.}$= total number of utterances containing t, $N_{.c}$= total number of utterances containing c, and N = total number of utterances.

To identify the most relevant lexical features, we extracted from the data all the transcribed user utterances. We removed all words that realize concepts (e.g. "61C", "Squirrel Hill"), as these are likely to be misrecognized in a post-confirmation utterance. We then extracted all word unigrams and bigrams. We computed the mutual information between each potential lexical feature and concept type. We then selected the 30 features with the highest mutual information which occurred at least 20 times in the training data[4].

For transcribed speech only, we also compute the string edit distance between the current and previous user utterances. This gives some indication of whether the current utterance is a correction or topic change (vs. a confirmation). However, for recognized speech recognition errors reduce the effectiveness of this feature (and of the concept features in the dialog history feature set).

4.3 Baseline

A simple baseline for this task, **No-Concept**, always predicts *none* in post-confirmation utterances. This baseline achieves overall classification accuracy of 82% but *rec+* of 0. At the other extreme, the **Confirmation State** baseline assigns to each utterance the dialog system's confirmation prompt type (using the DIA feature). This baseline achieves *rec+* of .79, but overall classification accuracy of only 14%. In all of the models used in our experiments, we include the current confirmation prompt type (DIA) feature.

4.4 Experiment Results

In this section we report the results of experiments on concept type classification in which we examine the impact of the feature sets presented in Table 3. We report performance separately for recognized speech, which is available at runtime (Table 5); and for transcribed speech, which gives us an idea of best possible performance (Table 4).

4.4.1 Features from the Current Utterance

We first look at lexical (LEX) and prosodic (RAW) features from the current utterance. For both recognized and transcribed speech, the LEX model achieves significantly higher *rec+* and overall accuracy than the RAW model ($p < .001$). For recognized speech, however, the LEX model has significantly more *switch+* errors than the RAW model ($p < .001$). This is not surprising since the majority of errors made by the RAW model are labeling an utterance with a concept as *none*. Utterances misclassified in this way are not subject to second-pass recognition and do not increase WER.

[4]We aimed to select equal number of features for each class with information measure in the top 25%. 30 was an empirically derived threshold for the number of lexical features to satisfy the desired condition.

Features	Place			Time			Bus			Overall					
	pre+	rec+	acc	pre+	rec+	acc	pre+	rec+	acc	pre+	rec+	f+	acc	switch+	switch
No Concept	0	0	.86	0	0	0.81	0	0	.92	0	0	0	**0.82**	0	0
Confirmation State	0.87	0.85	0.86	0.64	0.54	0.58	0.71	0.87	0.78	**0.14**	**0.79**	**0.24**	0.14	17	72.3
RAW	0.65	0.53	0.92	0.25	0.01	0.96	0.38	0.07	0.96	0.67	0.34	0.45	0.85	**6.43**	4.03
LEX	0.81	0.88	0.96	0.77	0.48	0.98	0.83	0.59	0.98	0.87	**0.72**	**0.79**	**0.93**	7.32	3.22
LEX_RAW	0.83	0.84	0.96	0.75	0.54	0.98	0.76	0.59	0.98	**0.88**	0.70	0.78	**0.93**	7.39	**3.00**
DH1_LEX	0.85	0.91	0.97	0.72	0.63	0.98	0.89	0.83	0.99	0.88	**0.81**	**0.84**	**0.95**	5.48	2.85
DH3_LEX	0.85	0.87	0.97	0.72	0.59	0.98	0.92	0.82	0.99	**0.89**	0.78	0.83	0.94	**5.22**	**2.62**

Table 4: Concept type classification results: transcribed speech (all models include feature DIA). Best overall values in each group are highlighted in bold.

Features	Place			Time			Bus			Overall					
	pre+	rec+	acc	pre+	rec+	acc	pre+	rec+	acc	pre+	rec+	f+	acc	switch+	switch
No Concept	0	0	.86	0	0	0.81	0	0	.92	0	0	0	**0.82**	**0**	**0**
Confirmation State	0.87	0.85	0.86	0.64	0.54	0.58	0.71	0.87	0.78	**0.14**	**0.79**	**0.24**	0.14	17	72.3
RAW	0.65	0.53	0.92	0.25	0.01	0.96	0.38	0.07	0.96	0.67	0.34	0.45	0.85	**6.43**	**4.03**
LEX	0.70	0.70	0.93	0.67	0.15	0.97	0.65	0.62	0.98	0.75	0.56	0.64	0.89	9.94	4.93
LEX_RAW	0.70	0.72	0.93	0.66	0.38	0.97	0.68	0.57	0.98	**0.76**	**0.60**	**0.67**	**0.90**	10.32	5.10
DH1_LEX_RAW	0.71	0.68	0.93	0.68	0.38	0.97	0.78	0.63	0.98	**0.77**	0.60	0.67	**0.90**	8.15	**4.55**
DH3_LEX_RAW	0.71	0.70	0.93	0.67	0.42	0.97	0.79	0.63	0.98	**0.77**	**0.62**	**0.68**	**0.90**	**7.20**	4.57
ASR_DH3_LEX _RAW	0.71	0.70	0.93	0.69	0.42	0.97	0.79	0.63	0.98	**0.77**	**0.62**	**0.68**	**0.90**	**7.20**	**4.54**
CTM_DH3_LEX _RAW	0.82	0.82	0.96	0.86	0.71	0.99	0.76	0.68	0.98	**0.85**	**0.74**	**0.79**	**0.93**	**3.89**	**2.94**
CTM_ASR_DH3 _LEX_RAW	0.82	0.81	0.96	0.86	0.69	0.99	0.76	0.68	0.98	**0.85**	**0.74**	**0.79**	**0.93**	4.27	3.01

Table 5: Concept type classification results: recognized speech (all models include feature DIA). Best overall values in each group are highlighted in bold.

For transcribed speech, the LEX_RAW model does not perform significantly differently from the LEX model in terms of overall accuracy, *rec+*, or *switch+* errors. However, for recognized speech, LEX_RAW achieves significantly higher *rec+* and overall accuracy than LEX ($p < .001$). Lexical content from transcribed speech is a very good indicator of concept type. However, lexical content from recognized speech is noisy, so concept type classification from ASR output can be improved by using acoustic/prosodic features.

We note that models containing only features from the current utterance perform significantly worse than the *confirmation state* baseline in terms of *rec+* ($p < .001$). However, they have significantly better overall accuracy and fewer *switch+* errors ($p < .001$) .

4.4.2 Features from the Dialog History

Next, we add features from the dialog history to our best-performing models so far. For transcribed speech, DH1_LEX performs significantly better than LEX in terms of overall accuracy, *rec+*, and *switch+* errors ($p < .001$). DH3_LEX performs significantly worse than DH1_LEX in terms of *rec+* ($p < 0.05$). For recognized speech, neither DH1_LEX_ RAW nor DH3_LEX_RAW is significantly different from LEX_RAW in terms of *rec+* or overall accuracy. However, both DH1_LEX_RAW and DH3_LEX_RAW do perform significantly better than LEX_RAW in terms of *switch+* errors ($p < .05$). There are no significant performance differences between DH1_LEX_RAW and DH3_LEX_RAW.

4.4.3 Features Specific to Recognized Speech

Finally, we add the ASR and CTM features to models trained on recognized speech.

We hypothesized that the classifier can use the recognizer's confidence score to decide whether an utterance is likely to have been misrecognized. However, ASR_DH3_LEX_RAW is not significantly different from DH3_LEX_RAW in terms of *rec+*, overall accuracy or *switch+* errors.

We hypothesized that the CTM feature will improve cases where a part of (but not the whole) concept instance is recognized in first-pass recognition[5]. The generic language model used in first-pass recognition recognizes some concept-related words. So, if in the utterance *Madison avenue*, *avenue* (but not *Madison*), is recognized in the first-pass recognition, the CTM feature can flag the utterance with a partial match for *place*, helping the classifier to correctly assign the *place*

[5]We do not try the CTM feature on transcribed speech because there is a one-to-one correspondence between presence of the concept and the CTM feature, so it perfectly indicates presence of a concept.

type to the utterance. Then, in the second-pass recognition the utterance will be decoded with a *place* concept-specific language model, potentially improving speech recognition performance. Adding the CTM feature to DH3_LEX_RAW and ASR_DH3_LEX_RAW leads to a large statistically significant improvement in all measures: a 12% absolute increase in *rec+*, a 3% absolute increase in overall accuracy, and decreases in *switch+* errors ($p < .001$). There are no statistically significant differences between these two models.

4.4.4 Summary and Discussion

In this section we evaluated different models for concept type classification. The best performing transcribed speech model, DH1_LEX, significantly outperforms the **Confirmation State** baseline on overall accuracy and on *switch+* and *switch* errors ($p < .001$), and is not significantly different on *rec+*. The best performing recognized speech model, CTM_DH3_LEX_RAW, significantly outperforms the **Confirmation State** baseline on overall accuracy and on *switch+* and *switch* errors, but is significantly worse on *rec+* ($p < .001$). The best transcribed speech model achieves significantly higher *rec+* and overall accuracy than the best recognized speech model ($p < .01$).

5 Speech Recognition Experiment

In this section we report the impact of concept type prediction on recognition of post-confirmation utterances in *Let's Go!* system data. We hypothesized that speech recognition performance for utterances containing a concept can be improved with the use of concept-specific LMs. We (1) compare the existing *dialog state-specific* LM adaptation approach used in *Let's Go!* with our proposed *concept-specific* adaptation; (2) compare two approaches to *concept-specific* adaptation (using the system's confirmation prompt type and using our concept type classifiers); and (3) evaluate the impact of different concept type classifiers on *concept-specific* LM adaptation.

5.1 Method

We used the PocketSphinx speech recognition engine (et al., 2006) with gender-specific telephone-quality acoustic models built for Communicator (et al., 2000). We trained trigram LMs using 0.5 ratio discounting with the CMU language modeling toolkit (Xu and Rudnicky, 2000)[6]. We built state- and concept-specific hierarchical LMs from the *Let's Go!* 2005 data. The LMs are built with *[place]*, *[time]* and *[bus]* submodels.

We evaluate speech recognition performance on the post-confirmation user utterances from the 2006 testing dataset. Each experiment varies in 1) the LM used for the final recognition pass and 2) the method of selecting a LM for use in decoding.

5.1.1 Language models

We built seven LMs for these experiments. The *state-specific* LM contains all utterances in the training data that were produced in the *yes-no* dialog state. The *confirm-place*, *confirm-bus* and *confirm-time* LMs contain all utterances produced in the *yes-no* dialog state following *confirm_place*, *confirm_bus* and *confirm_time* system confirmation prompts respectively. Finally, the *concept-place*, *concept-bus* and *concept-time* LMs contain all utterances produced in the *yes-no* dialog state that contain a mention of a *place*, *bus* or *time*.

5.1.2 Decoders

In the baseline, **1-pass general** condition, we use the *state-specific* LM to recognize all post-confirmation utterances. In the **1-pass state** experimental condition we use the *confirm-place, confirm-bus* and *confirm-time* LMs to recognize testing utterances produced following a *confirm_place*, *confirm_bus* and *confirm_time* prompt respectively[7]. In the **1-pass concept** experimental condition we use the *concept-place, concept-bus* and *concept-time* LMs to recognize testing utterances produced following a *confirm_place*, *confirm_bus* and *confirm_time* prompt respectively.

In the *2-pass* conditions we perform first-pass recognition using the *general* LM. Then, we classify the output of the first pass using a concept type classifier. Finally, we perform second-pass recognition using the *concept-place, concept-bus* or *concept-time* LMs if the utterance was classified as *place, bus* or *time* respectively[8]. We used the three classification models with highest overall *rec+*: DH3_LEX_RAW, ASR_DH3_LEX_RAW,

[6]We chose the same speech recognizer, acoustic models, language modeling toolkit, and LM building parameters that are used in the live *Let's Go!* system (Raux et al., 2005).

[7]As we showed in Table 2, most, but not all, utterances in a confirmation state contain the corresponding concept.

[8]We treat utterances classified as containing more than concept type as *none*. In the 2006 data, only 5.6% of utterances with a concept contain more than one concept type.

Recognizer	Concept type classifier	Language model	Overall	Concept utterances	
			WER	WER	Concept recall
1-pass	general	state-specific	38.49%	49.12%	50.75%
1-pass	confirm state	confirm-{place,bus,time}	38.83%	48.96%	51.36%
1-pass	confirm state	concept-{place,bus,time}, state-specific	46.47% ♠	50.73% ♣	52.9% *
2-pass	**DH3_LEX_RAW**	concept-{place,bus,time}, state-specific	38.48%	47.56% ♠	53.2% *
2-pass	**ASR_DH3_LEX_RAW**	concept-{place,bus,time}, state-specific	38.51%	47.99% ♣	52.7%
2-pass	**CTM_ASR_DH3_LEX_RAW**	concept-{place,bus,time}, state-specific	38.42%	47.86% ♣	52.6%
2-pass	oracle	concept-{place,bus,time}, state-specific	37.85% ♠	45.94% ♠	54.91% ♠

Table 6: Speech recognition results. ♠ indicates significant difference (p<.01). ♣ indicates significant difference (p<.05). * indicates near-significant trend in difference (p<.07). Significance for WER is computed as a paired t-test. Significance for concept recall is an inference on proportion.

and CTM_ASR_DH3_LEX_RAW. To get an idea of "best possible" performance, we also report 2-pass oracle recognition results, assuming an oracle classifier that always outputs the correct concept type for an utterance.

5.2 Results

In Table 6 we report average per-utterance word error rate (WER) on post-confirmation utterances, average per-utterance WER on post-confirmation utterances containing a concept, and average concept recall rate (percentage of correctly recognized concepts) on post-confirmation utterances containing a concept. In slot-filling dialog systems like *Let's Go!*, the concept recall rate largely determines the potential of the system to understand user-provided information and continue the dialog successfully. Our goal is to maximize concept recall and minimize concept utterance WER, without causing overall WER to decline.

As Table 6 shows, the **1-pass state** and **1-pass concept** recognizers perform better than the **1-pass general** recognizer in terms of concept recall, but worse in terms of overall WER. Most of these differences are not statistically significant. However, the **1-pass concept** recognizer has significantly worse overall and concept utterance WER than the **1-pass general** recognizer ($p < .01$).

All of the 2-pass recognizers that use automatic concept prediction achieve significantly lower concept utterance WER than the **1-pass general** recognizer ($p < .05$). Differences between these recognizers in overall WER and concept recall are not significant.

The **2-pass oracle** recognizer achieves significantly higher concept recall and significantly lower overall and concept utterance WER than the **1-pass general** recognizer ($p < .01$). It also achieves significantly lower concept utterance WER than any of the 2-pass recognizers that use automatic concept prediction ($p < .01$).

Our **2-pass concept** results show that it is possible to use knowledge of the concepts in a user's utterance to improve speech recognition. Our **1-pass concept** results show that this cannot be effectively done by assuming that the user will always address the system's question; instead, one must consider the user's actual utterance and the discourse history (as in our DH3_LEX_RAW model).

6 Conclusions and Future Work

In this paper, we examined user responses to system confirmation prompts in task-oriented spoken dialog. We showed that these post-confirmation utterances may contain unrequested task-relevant concepts that are likely to be misrecognized. Using acoustic, lexical, dialog state and dialog history features, we were able to classify task-relevant concepts in the ASR output for post-confirmation utterances with 90% accuracy. We showed that use of a concept type classifier can lead to improvements in speech recognition performance in terms of WER and concept recall.

Of course, any possible improvements in speech recognition performance are dependent on (1) the performance of concept type classification; (2) the accuracy of the first-pass speech recognition; and (3) the accuracy of the second-pass speech recognition. For example, with our general language model, we get a fairly high overall WER of 38.49%. In future work, we will systematically vary the WER of both the first- and second-pass speech recognizers to further explore the interaction between speech recognition performance and concept type classification.

The improvements our two-pass recognizers achieve have quite small local effects (up to 3.18% absolute improvement in WER on utterances containing a concept, and less than 1% on post-confirmation utterances overall) but may have larger impact on dialog completion times and task completion rates, as they reduce the number of cascading recognition errors in the dialog (et al., 2002). Furthermore, we could also use knowledge of the concept type(s) contained in a user utterance to improve dialog management and response planning (Bohus, 2007). In future work, we will look at (1) extending the use of our concept-type classifiers to utterances following any system prompt; and (2) the impact of these interventions on overall metrics of dialog success.

7 Acknowledgements

We would like to thank the researchers at CMU for providing the *Let's Go!* data and additional resources.

References

J. R. Bellegarda. 2004. Statistical language model adaptation: Review and perspectives. *Speech Communication Special Issue on Adaptation Methods for Speech Recognition*, 42:93–108.

D. Bohus. 2007. *Error awareness and recovery in task-oriented spoken dialog systems*. Ph.D. thesis, Carnegie Mellon University.

Y. Esteve, F. Bechet, A. Nasr, and R. Mori. 2001. Stochastic finite state automata language model triggered by dialogue states. In *Proceedings of Eurospeech*.

A. Rudnicky et al. 2000. Task and domain specific modelling in the Carnegie Mellon Communicator system. In *Proceedings of ICSLP*.

J. Shin et al. 2002. Analysis of user behavior under error conditions in spoken dialogs. In *Proceedings of ICSLP*.

D. Huggins-Daines et al. 2006. Sphinx: A free, real-time continuous speech recognition system for handheld devices. In *Proceedings of ICASSP*.

D. Gildea and T. Hofmann. 1999. Topic-based language models using EM. In *Proceedings of Eurospeech*.

J. Hirschberg, D. Litman, and M. Swerts. 2004. Prosodic and other cues to speech recognition failures. *Speech Communication*, 43:155–175.

R. Iyer and M. Ostendorf. 1999. Modeling long distance dependencies in language: Topic mixtures versus dynamic cache model. *IEEE Transactions on Speech and Audio Processing*, 7(1):30–39.

E. Krahmer, M. Swerts, M. Theune, and M. Weegels. 2001. Error detection in spoken human-machine interaction. *International Journal of Speech Technology*, 4(1).

G.-A. Levow. 1998. Characterizing and recognizing spoken corrections in human-computer dialogue. In *Proceedings of COLING-ACL*.

D. Litman, J.Hirschberg, and M. Swerts. 2006. Characterizing and predicting corrections in spoken dialogue systems. *Computational Linguistics*, 32:417–438.

C. D. Manning, P. Raghavan, and H. Schütze. 2008. *Introduction to Information Retrieval*. Cambridge University Press.

A. Raux, B. Langner, A. Black, and M Eskenazi. 2005. Let's Go Public! Taking a spoken dialog system to the real world. In *Proceedings of Eurospeech*.

G. Riccardi and A. L. Gorin. 2000. Stochastic language adaptation over time and state in a natural spoken dialog system. *IEEE Transactions on Speech and Audio Processing*, 8(1):3–9.

S. Stenchikova, D. Hakkani-Tür, and G. Tur. 2008. Name-aware speech recognition for interactive question answering. In *Proceedings of ICASSP*.

G. Tur and A. Stolcke. 2007. Unsupervised language model adaptation for meeting recognition. In *Proceedings of ICASSP*.

G. Tur. 2005. Model adaptation for spoken language understanding. In *Proceedings of ICASSP*.

G. Tur. 2007. Extending boosting for large scale spoken language understanding. *Machine Learning*, 69(1):55–74.

M. Walker, J. Wright, and I. Langkilde. 2000. Using natural language processing and discourse features to identify understanding errors in a spoken dialogue system. In *Proceedings of ICML*.

I. Witten and E. Frank. 2005. *Data Mining: Practical machine learning tools and techniques*. Morgan Kaufmann, San Francisco, 2nd edition.

W. Xu and A. Rudnicky. 2000. Language modeling for dialog system. In *Proceedings of ICSLP*.

S. Young. 1994. Detecting misrecognitions and out-of-vocabulary words. In *Proceedings of ICASSP*.

Deeper spoken language understanding for man-machine dialogue on broader application domains: a logical alternative to concept spotting

Jeanne Villaneau
UEB (Université Européenne de Bretagne)
VALORIA
France
villanea@univ-ubs.fr

Jean-Yves Antoine
Université François Rabelais - Tours
LI
France
Jean-Yves.Antoine@univ-tours.fr

Abstract

LOGUS is a French-speaking spoken language understanding (SLU) system which carries out a deeper analysis than those achieved by standard concept spotters. It is designed for multi-domain conversational systems or for systems that are working on complex application domains. Based on a logical approach, the system adapts the ideas of incremental robust parsing to the issue of SLU. The paper provides a detailed description of the system as well as results from two evaluation campaigns that concerned all of current French-speaking SLU systems. The observed error rates suggest that our logical approach can stand comparison with concept spotters on restricted application domains, but also that its behaviour is promising for larger domains. The question of the generality of the approach is precisely addressed by our current investigations on a new task: SLU for an emotional robot companion for young hospital patents.

1 Introduction

Despite the indisputable advances of automatic speech recognition (ASR), highly spontaneous speech remains an important barrier to the wide spreading of speech based applications. The goal of spontaneous speech understanding remains feasible, provided the interaction between the user and the system is restricted to a task-oriented dialogue (restricted vocabulary). Present research is investigating mixed or user initiated dialogue for less restricted tasks. It is the purpose of this paper, which focuses on spontaneous speech understanding in such complex applications.

Generally speaking, information speech dialogue systems are based on the same architecture. At first, a speech recognizer processes the speech signal and provides a string (or a lattice) of words that should correspond to the spoken sentence. Then, this string is parsed by a spoken language understanding module (SLU) in order to build a semantic representation that represents its propositional meaning. Finally, this semantic structure is sent to a dialogue manager which controls the interaction with the user (database interrogation, dialogue management, answer generation). The answers to the user can be displayed on screen and/or through a message generated by a text-to-speech synthesis. This paper focuses on the SLU module of such a dialogue system. On the whole, SLU has to cope with two main difficulties:

- speech recognition errors: highly spontaneous speech remains hard to recognize for current ASR systems (Zue et al., 2000). Therefore, the SLU module has to work on a strongly corrupted string of words.
- spoken disfluencies: filled pauses, repetitions and repairs make the parsing of conversational spoken language significantly harder to achieve (Heeman, Allen, 2001).

In order to overcome those difficulties, most SLU systems follow a selective strategy which comes down to a simple concept spotting: they restrict the semantic analysis to a mapping of the sentence with the main expectations of the user in relation with the task (Minker W. et al., 1999; Bangalore S. et al., 2006). Consider, for instance, an air transport information system and the following spoken utterance:

(1) *Cou- could you list me the flights uh the scheduled flights for Tenerife Tenerife Tenerife North please*

Satisfying the speaker's goals only requires detecting the nature of their requests (list flights) and the required destination (Tenerife North). Those

Proceedings of EACL 2009 Workshop on Semantic Representation of Spoken Language - SRSL 2009, pages 50–57,
Athens, Greece, 30 March 2009. ©2009 Association for Computational Linguistics

two concepts (list, Tenerife North) will fill a shallow semantic frame which is supposed to represent the useful meaning of the sentence. Such task-driven approaches meet, to a great extent, the needs of SLU in terms of robustness, since they only involve a partial analysis of the sentence. Whether the processing is based on a statistical or a knowledge-based approach, several evaluation campaigns proved that concept spotting is suitable for spoken language understanding, provided the application task is sufficiently restricted. However, concept spotters suffer from noticeable limitations:

- Although they resist gracefully speech recognition errors, they are not able to detect their eventual presence, since they do not consider the global structure of the sentence. This limitation can be particularly penalizing when the error is related to a key element, for example when the error prevents the system to determine the type (dialogue act) of the utterance. Indeed, concept spotters often base SLU on the initial characterization of the question type. When analyzing the errors of his statistical concept spotter, Minker has shown that the correct identification of the question type is a key issue in terms of final robustness (Minker W. et al., 1999).

- Since they are based on the identification of rather flat semantic frames, these approaches hardly succeed in representing complex syntactic relations such as overlapping coordinate phrases or negations.

- Although it is well known that generality is an important issue for SLU, this question is generally approached in term of technical portability from one (narrow) task to another. Now, one should wonder whether concept spotting is still suitable on larger application domains. It seems that the robustness of the spotting process depends strongly on the degree of lexical ambiguity of the considered task. For instance, Bousquet has shown that the concept error rate of her stochastic spotter is two times higher on ambiguous words than on non ambiguous ones (Bousquet et al., 2003).

Such considerations tend to show that to apply concept spotting to more complex tasks could be difficult. Such observations are well known (Zechner K., 1998; Van Noord et al., 1999), and noticeable attempts have already been done to reach a deeper semantic analysis. However, statistical or knowledge-based concept spotting remains the prevailing paradigm in SLU, mainly because of engineering motivations (quick and easy building). On the contrary, we have decided to develop a SLU system (LOGUS[1]) which carries out a complete analysis of the utterance while keeping the robustness of standard concept spotting approaches. The system, which is based on a logical approach, adapts the ideas of incremental robust parsing (Aït-Mokhtar S., 2002; Basili, 2003) to the issue of speech conversational systems. In section 2, we will describe the system into detail. Then, section 3 will present results from different evaluation campaigns in which we participated. These experiments concerned standard restricted tasks (hotel reservation for instance) for which concept spotting is well adapted. As a result, this section does not aim to prove a superiority of our approach, but simply to show that this deeper processing is able to keep a satisfactory robustness, by comparison with prevailing approaches. Finally, we give in section 4 a brief description on our present work concerning the integration of LOGUS in a conversational robot which is dedicated to general interaction with children who are in hospital for a long-stay. This example will illustrate the portability abilities of our approach on complex application tasks, in addition with our previous works on general tourism information.

2 Description of the LOGUS system

The task of a SLU is to turn a sequence or a graph of words into a semantic representation; so a SLU system has to perform a translation from natural language to a formal target language. This section begins with the description of the formal language chosen for the LOGUS system. We then explain the basic principles of parsing and its main steps.

2.1 Semantic representation

When it comes to the choice of a target language for the system, the following points must be taken into account.

- We want to implement automatic understanding in application domains where predefined

[1] LOGical Understanding System.

semantic frames are not sufficient to represent all the possible queries (Van Noord et al., 1999). Furthermore, any SLU aims at providing results usable by a dialogue manager: the target language must reconcile simplicity with precision.

- This semantic representation must obviously extend to a pragmatic one. That means that it should involve the characterization of the dialogue acts related to the speech turn (Austin J.-L., 1962).

We have chosen a formalism compatible with these constraints and inspired by the illocutionary logic of D. Vanderveken (Vanderveken D., 1981). In this formalism, the form of an elementary illocutionary act is *F(P)* where F is the illocutionary force, and P its propositional content.

The LOGUS system thus provides a logical formula as the semantic representation of an utterance. A *language act* contains clues about the intentions of the speaker: it is labelled illocutionary force, while the propositional content is a structure built with the domain objects and their properties which is called an *object string*.

The following example shows a single speech turn uttered for a tourism information system:

(2) *j'ai réservé une chambre dans un deux étoiles l'hôtel euh l'hôtel Rex pour y aller d'ici comment est-ce que je peux faire (I booked a room in a two-star hotel in the hotel hum in the Rex hotel from here how can I go at there)*

This turn expresses two different language acts, which is quite usual in conversational speech: a piece of information *(I booked a room...)* is followed by the user question *(... how can I go....* Such complex speech turns are difficult to analyze for concept spotters, since they usually base the parsing on one language act detection. The logical formula LOGUS provides is split into two language acts: *(information act)* and *(question how)*. The second act is interpreted by the system in the context of the first one:

((information act)
(of (reservation [])
(hotel [(ident. (name "Rex")),(star (int 2))])))
((question how)
(to_go [(to (contextual_location [])),
(from (hotel [(ident. (name "Rex"))]))]))

In the formula, *reservation, hotel* and *to_go* are object labels; *(ident. (name "Rex")), (star (int 2))* are properties. The two objects of labels *reservation* and *hotel* are linked with the generic relation *of*, which indicates a subordination relation. It is the main relation, (in addition with logical coordinations *and, or* and *not*) which is used for building complex object strings.

2.2 General system architecture

Incremental parsing methodology is used for text parsing in order to combine efficiency with robustness (Aït-Mokhtar S., 2002). With LOGUS, we tried to show that such methods can be extended to spoken language parsing.

The system has to parse out-of-grammar constructions but spoken language studies have shown that minimal syntactic structures are generally preserved in repairs and false-starts (Mc Kelvie D., 1998). We have thus chosen to carry out an incremental bottom-up parsing, where words are gradually combined. At the beginning, the parser groups words according to mainly syntactic rules in order to form minimal chunks that correspond to basic concepts of the application domain. Then, as word group size increases, their meaning becomes more precise, enough to relax syntactic criteria and thereby overcome the problem of out-of-grammar sentences.

The general architecture of the system is shown in Figure 1. The parsing is essentially split into three stages. The first stage is *chunking* (Abney S., 1991) where grammatical words are linked to the lexical words to which they are referred. The following stage gradually builds links between the chunks in order to detect semantic relations between the corresponding concepts, and the last one achieves a contextual interpretation (anaphoric resolution for instance). The process of building links between chunks and contextual understanding uses a domain ontology.

Only one formalism is used during these parsing stages. It is designed to distinguish syntax and semantics and to preserve genericity of the parsing rules. Each component is specified by a list of what we can call definitions; each of them is a triplet $< C, R, T >$ where

C: is a syntactic label, called *syntactic category*: for example *adjective, (verb 1 present)*.

R: points out the semantic function of the component. It is called *semantic role*: for example *object, (prop price)* where *prop* is for property.

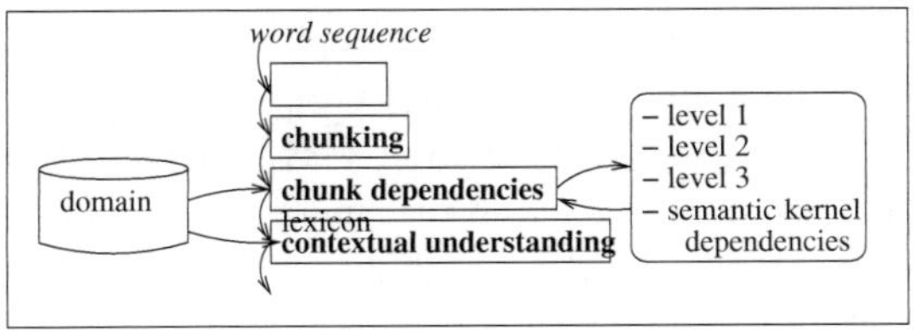

Figure 1: General architecture of the LOGUS system

T: is the *semantic translation*. It is an element of the logical formula built by the system. It belongs thus to the target language.

The first two triplet elements, C and R, are widely domain independent. A basic principle is to define parsing rules from these elements in order to preserve the genericity of the system. Each parsing rule combines two or three triplets in order to build a new result triplet.

2.3 Chunking

Our experiments with LOGUS have clearly shown that *chunking* is effective for spoken language, provided the chunks are very short: more precisely, errors made at the speech recognition level make it dangerous to link objects or properties according to pure syntactic criteria, without checking these links with semantic criteria. Therefore the *chunks* built by LOGUS include only one content word: we call them *minimal chunks*. *Chunking* is based on the principle of linking function words to the near content word.

The formalism used in this step is inspired by Categorial Grammars of the AB type[2], whose rules are generalized from the first two elements of the constituent triplets. Function words have definitions in which syntactic category and semantic role are fractional. In such definitions, the semantic translation is a λ-abstraction (in the λ-calculus meaning)[3]. The semantic translation of the result triplet is achieved by applying this abstraction to the semantic translation of the un-fractional triplet. Formally, the following two rules are applied, where F is an abstraction:

$$< C_A/C_B,\ R_A/R_B,\ F >,\ < C_B,\ R_B,\ S_B > \\ \rightarrow < C_A,\ R_A,\ (F\ S_B) >$$

$$< C_B,\ R_B,\ S_B >, < C_B\backslash C_A,\ R_B\backslash R_A,\ F > \\ \rightarrow < C_A,\ R_A,\ (F\ S_B) >$$

[2]The formalism can be expressed in terms of pregroup formalism too (Lambek J., 1999).

[3]LOGUS is implemented in λProlog, a logic programming language whose terms are λ-terms with simple types.

In the following example only one definition is shown for each component (*gn* is for *nominal group*).

	trois (three)	*étoiles (stars)*
C	adj_num	adj_num\gn
R	(prop nb)	(prop nb)\(prop nb_star)
S	(int 3)	λx.(star x)

By applying the second rule, we obtain the following chunk:

"trois étoiles" (three stars)
<gn, (prop nb_star), (star (int 3))>.

The semantic translation of the result triplet is obtained by β-reduction of the λ-term *(λx. (star x) (int 3))*. For example, the utterance

(3) *"À l'hôtel Caumartin quels sont le les tarifs pour pour une chambre double" (In Caumartin hotel what are the the prices for for a double room)* is segmented into six chunks during the *chunking* stage. Their semantic translations are:

[1] *(hotel [])*,
[2] *(identity (name "Caumartin"))])*,
[3] *(what (interrogation))*, [4] *(price [])*,
[5] *(room [])*, [6] *(size double)*.

At the end of the *chunking* process, the determiner *le* and the first occurrence of the preposition *pour* are deleted because they are fragments without semantic content. Deletions such as these are a first way of dealing with repairs.

2.4 Domain ontology

The limited scope of the application domain makes it possible to describe exhaustively the pragmatic and semantic domain knowledge. A domain ontology specifies how objects and properties can be compounded. The handled processings are expected to be generic while using a domain dependent ontology: to achieve that, the ontology is defined by generic predicates whose domain objects and domain properties are the arguments.

For example, the possibility of building the conceptual relation *of* between two objects (cf. 2.1) is defined by the predicate *is_sub_object* whose arguments are two object labels: so the relation *is_sub_object(room, hotel)* expresses a part-whole relation possibility between such two objects.

2.5 Chunk dependencies

Chunk dependencies are built by an incremental process which is compound of several successive stages. Each stage is based on rewriting rules which are specified from the first two components of the constituent triplets and from the generic ontology predicates. They are thus not specific to the domain of application, what assures, to a certain extent, the genericity of the process.

Consider for instance the following rule, which leads to the binding of two consecutive chunks which share a meronomic (part_of) relation:

$$\frac{\begin{array}{l} < C_1,\ object,\ O_1 >,\ < C_2,\ object,\ O_2 > \\ \text{- } O_1 \textit{ simple object of label } Et_1 \\ \text{- } O_2 \textit{ object string of label } Et_2 \\ \text{- } \textit{is\_sub\_object}(Et_1,\ Et_2) \end{array}}{< C,\ object,\ (of\ O_1\ O_2) >}$$

where C *is obtained by composing* C_1 *and* C_2.

As an illustration, this rule will form a complex object *(of (price []) (room [(size double)]))* from the initial two chunks *(price [])* and *(room (size double))*. This rule is completely generic and should apply on any task. The knowledge specific to the task intervenes only on the definition of the predicate *is_sub_object*. As a result, one could speak of procedural genericity to qualify our system.

As long as possible, the first processing stages try to respect syntactic criteria. However, in presence of spoken disfluencies or speech recognition errors, it is likely that the utterance is out-of-grammar. Therefore, since the detected links between chunks make the meaning of the linked chunks more specific, the next stage tries to detect chunk dependencies more on more on semantic or pragmatic features only. Subsequently, studying dependencies between the components makes it possible to eliminate some components, especially in the case of word recognition errors.

As an illustration, Figure 2 shows how links are gradually built during the parsing stage of utterance (3) (cf. section 2.3). The chunks are in rectangular boxes in dotted lines.

The first step of chunk binding links the first two chunks into the object:

(hotel [(ident. (name "Caumartin"))]).

The second step links the object *(room [])* with the property *(size (double))* to obtain the object *(room [(size double)])*. Then, the two objects *price* and *room* are linked with the conceptual relation *of* to obtain *(of (price []) (room [(size double)]))* and this object string is connected to the language act: *(question what)*. The position of the prepositional phrase *à l'hotel Caumartin* is not usual in French syntagmatic ordering. It is indeed an example of extraposition which is not accepted by the syntactic constraints considered by the system. As a result, the conceptual relation *of*, which links the object of label *room* with the object *(hotel [ident. (name "Caumartin")])* is built later, when these constraints are relaxed.

2.6 Contextual understanding

Many sentences are elliptical and incomplete in a dialogue. Therefore, it is necessary to use the current context of the task and the dialogue history in order to complete their understanding. The objectives of the contextual understanding in LOGUS are thus close to the objectives of the authors of the OntoSem system (McShane M., 2005): the completion of semantic fragments. Reference resolution is thereby extended to a more general completion of the semantic representation.

While syntactic anaphora criteria are generally respected in texts, anaphora gender and number are frequently broken in spoken language. Moreover, gender and number morphological marks are hardly perceptible in spoken French. They are therefore very often corrupted by speech recognition errors. So, in the LOGUS system, anaphora resolution is based on the same principles as the rest of the parsing: combining syntactic and semantic criteria. Both nominal and pronominal anaphora (with definite expressions) are considered during this contextual interpretation stage.

Completion is based on the concept of *object string*. A property or an object may be completed by an "over-object" of the context, if the ontology makes it possible to do so. For example, the object *price* of the sentence *"quel est le tarif" (what is the price)* is automatically completed in *(of (price []) (of (room []) (hotel [(name "Rex")]))* if the *object string (of (room []) (hotel [(name "Rex")]))* is an *object string* which is part of the previous utterance.

3 Evaluations and results

LOGUS is a French-speaking system. It took part in the two evaluation campaigns that were carried out in the last year designed for French spoken language understanding: the GDR-I3 challenge-based campaign and the MEDIA project.

3.1 The GDR-I3 campaign

LOGUS took part in the challenge-based campaign, held by the GDR-I3 consortium of the

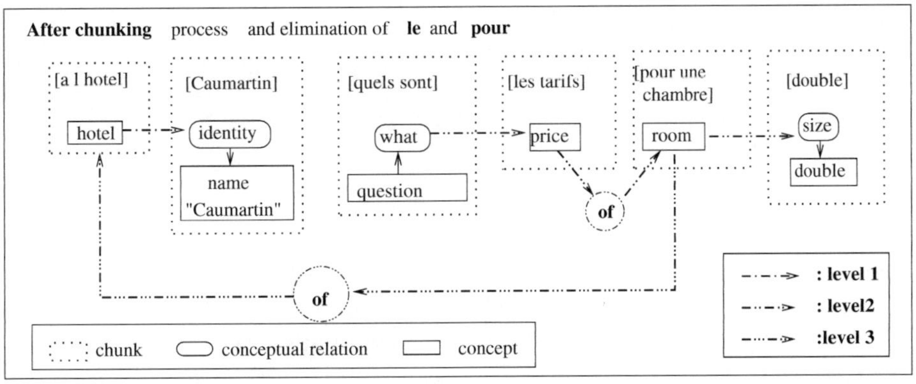

Figure 2: Characterization of chunk dependencies : example on the utterance *" à l'hotel Caumartin quels sont le les tarifs pour pour une chambre double" (in Caumartin hotel what are the the prices for for a double room.*

French CNRS research agency (Antoine et al., 2002). We won't describe here in detail the results of this campaign, since it concerned a former version of LOGUS. It seems however interesting to analyse the distribution of the errors made by LOGUS to have an idea of the benefits of our approach. The evaluation corpus was divided among several tests which were respectively related to a specific difficulty: speech recognition errors, speech repairs and other disfluences, and finally messages of a structural complexity (embedded coordination or subordination, for instance) significantly higher than those usually met in standard ATIS-like application domains.

The distribution of the concept error rates of the LOGUS SLU system is the following:

Speech recognition:	9.5%
Complex structures:	9.8%
Repairs:	15%

It should be noted here that the robustness of LOGUS decreases rather gracefully on complex messages, while SLU systems based on concept spotting meet real difficulties on such utterances. For instance, Cacao (Bousquet-Vernhettes et al., 1999; Bousquet-Vernhettes et al., 2003) is a concept spotter which participated to the GDR-I3 campaign. It has been shown that most of its errors resulted from its difficulties to resolve lexical ambiguities in complex sentences. This observation suggests that our logical deep parsing should fulfill better than concept spotting the needs of complex application domains such as general purpose tourist information or collaborative planning (Allen J. et al., 2002), or even multi-domain applications (Dzikovska M. et al., 2005). Unfortunatedly, French evaluation campaigns have never investigated such difficult tasks.

3.2 The MEDIA project

MEDIA-EVALDA was an evaluation campaign hold by the French Ministry of Research. It concerned all the French laboratory working on SLU. Once again, this evaluation investigated a rather restricted application domain: hotel reservation. It is well known that concept spotters fit succesfully such simple tasks. Nevertheless, we decided to take part in this evaluation in order to see to which extent LOGUS should be compared to standard concept spotters in such disavantageous conditions.

Participants defined reservation scenarios which were used to build a corpus made up of 1250 recorded dialogues. Recording used a WOZ system simulating vocal tourist phone server (Devillers et al., 2004). The MEDIA corpus, which is made up of real-life French spontaneous dialogues, is surely to become a benchmark reference for French contextual SLU.

The evaluation paradigm forced every participant to convert his own semantic representation into a common reference, which relies-on an attribute/value frame: each utterance is divided into semantic segments, aligned on the sentence, and each segment is represented by a triplet: (mode, attribute, value). Relations between attributes are represented by their order in the representation and the composed attribute names.

Nine systems participated to this first campaign. An error was count for any difference with one of the elements of the reference (mode, attribute

System	1	2	3	4 (LOGUS)	5
Approach	concept spotting	concept spotting	syntactic deep parsing	logical deep parsing	concept spotting
Error rate	29.0%	30.3%	36.3%	37.8%	41.3%

Table 1: MEDIA results.

or value). Table 1 summarises the results of the best five systems. At first glance, one should find the reported error rates rather deceptive. However, one must realize that the test corpus involved highly spontaneous conversational speech, with very frequent speech disfluences. As a result, these results should be compared, for instance, to ASR errors rates observed on the SWITCHBOARD corpus (Greenberg S. et al., 2000).

LOGUS was ranked fourth and its robustness was rather close to the best participants. Now, if you consider that the systems ranked 1st, 2nd and 5th were using a concept spotter, these results shows that our approach can bear comparison with standard approaches even on this task. These encouraging performances suggest that it is possible to achieve a deep understanding of conversational speech while respecting at the same time some robustness requirements: our approach seems indeed competitive even in a domain where concept spotters are known to be very efficient. To our mind, the interest of our approach is that this robustness should remain on larger application domains. We are precisely trying to test this genericity by adapting LOGUS to a wider application domain in the framework of the Emotirob project.

4 Genericity and portability experiment

We are currently testing the portability of our approach by adapting LOGUS to a really different task, which corresponds to an unrestricted application domain, general purpose understanding of child language, with additional emotional state detection. The whole project, supported by ANR (National French Research Agency), aims at achieving a robot companion which can interact with sick or disabled young children with the help of facial expressions. Although the robot does not have to react to every speech act of the child, we have to deal with spoken understanding in an unrestricted domain. Fortunately, the age of the children involved (3-5) implies a restricted vocabulary. This work is still in progress. Our first investigations suggest however that LOGUS is a suitable understanding system for the pursued purpose: since there will never be significant corpora related to this kind of task, we can't use statistical methods. Moreover, because of the genericity of LOGUS, the main part of the analysis can be reused without important changes. Thus, three-month work was enough to build a first prototype of the system and the problem is restricted to the main problem of this project: building an ontology which models the cognitive and emotional world of young children.

The generality of the used formalism makes it possible to include an emotional component by turning the triplet structure into a quadruplet structure. Of course, composition rules have to include this new component. We are currently working on the computation of the emotional states from both prosodic and lexical cues. Whereas many works have investigated a prosodic-based detection (Devillers et al., 2005), word-based approaches remain quite original. Our hypothesis is that emotion is compositional, e.g. that is possible to compute the global emotion carried by a sentence from the emotion of every content word. This calculation depends obviously of the semantic structure of the utterance: our system will precisely benefit from the characterization of the chunk dependencies carried on by LOGUS. For the moment being, we are working on the definition of a complete lexical norm of emotional values from children of 3, 5 and 7 years. This norm will be established in collaboration with psycholinguists from Montpellier University, France.

5 Conclusion

When we started implementing the LOGUS system, one of our objectives was to achieve robust parsing of spontaneous spoken language while making the application domain much wider than is currently done. Logical formalisms are not usually viewed as efficient tools for pragmatic applications. The promising results of LOGUS show that they can be brought into interesting new approaches.

Another objective was to have a rather generic system, despite the use of a domain-based semantic knowledge. We have fulfilled this constraint through the definition of generic predicates as well as generic rules working on semantic triplets or quadruplets which makes it possible to have generic chunk linking rules. The performances of LOGUS show that a deeper understanding can bear comparison with concept spotting approaches.

References

Abney S. 1991. Parsing by Chunks. *Principle Based Parsing*. R. Berwick, S. Abney and C. Tenny Eds. Kluwer Academix Publishers.

Aït-Mokhtar S., Chanod J.-P. and Roux C. 2002. Robustness beyond Shallowness: Incremental Deep Parsing. *Natural Language Engineering*, 8 (2-3): p. 121–144.

Allen J. and Ferguson G. 2002. Human-Machine Collaborative Planning. *Proc. of the 3rd International NASA Workshop on Planning and Scheduling for Space*, Houston, TX.

Antoine J.-Y. et al. 2002. Predictive and Objective Evaluation of Speech Understanding: the "challenge" evaluation campaign of the I3 speech workgroup of the french CNRS. *Proceedings of the LREC 2002, 3rd International Conference on Language Resources and Evaluation*, Las Palmas, Spain.

Austin J.-L. 1962. *How to do things with words*. Oxford.

Bangalore S., Hakkani-Tür D. and Tür G. 2006. *Special issue on Spoken Language Understanding in Conversational Systems*. Speech Communication. 48.

Basili R. and Zanzotto F.M. 2003. Parsing engineering and empirical robustness. *Natural Language Engineering*. 8 (2-3).

Bousquet-Vernhettes C., Bouraoui J.-L. and Vigouroux N. 2003. Language Model Study for Speech Understanding. *Proc. Internationnal Workshop on Speech and Computer (SPECOM'2003)* , Moscow, Russia, p. 205–208.

Bousquet-Vernhettes C., Privat R. and Vigouroux N. 2003. Error handling in spoken dialogue systems: toward corrective dialogue. *ISCA workshop on Error Handling in Spoken Dialogue Systems*, Chteau-d'Oex-Vaud, Suisse, p. 41–45.

Bousquet-Vernhettes C., Vigouroux N. and Pérennou G. 1999. Stochastic Conceptual Model for Spoken Language Understanding. *Proc. Internationnal Workshop on Speech and Computer (SPECOM'99)* , Moscow, Russia, p. 71–74.

Devillers L. et al. 2004. The French Evalda-Media project: the evaluation of the understanding capabilities of Spoken Language Dialogue Systems. *Proceedings of the LREC 2004, 4rd International Conference on Language Resources and Evaluation,* Lisboa, Portugal.

Devillers L., Vidrascu, L. and Lamel, L. 2005. Challenges in real-life emotion annotation and machine learning based detection. *Neural Networks*, 18, p. 407-422.

Dzikovska M., Swift M. and Allen J. and de Beaumont W. 2005. Generic parsing for multi-domain semantic interpretation. *Proc. 9th International Workshop on Parsing Technologies (IWPT05))*, Vancouver BC.

Greenberg S. and Chang, S. 2000. Linguistic dissection of switchboard-corpus automatic speech recognition systems. *Proc. ISCA Workshop on Automatic Speech Recognition: Challenges for the New Millennium*, Paris, France.

Heeman P. and Allen J. 2001. Improving robustness by modeling spontaneous events. *Robustness in language and speech technology*, Kluwer Academics. Dordrecht, NL. p. 123–152.

Lambek J. 1999. Type grammars revisited. *Logical Aspects of Computational Linguistics*, A. Lecomte, F. Lamarche and G. Perrier (eds), LNAI 1582, Springer, Berlin, p. 1–27.

Mc Kelvie D. 1998. The syntax of disfluency in spontaneous spoken language. *HCRC Research Paper*, HCRC/RP-95.

McShane M. 2005. Semantics-based resolution of fragments and underspecified structures. *Traitement Automatique des Langues*, 46(1): p. 163–184.

Minker W., Waibel A. and Mariani J.. 1999. *Stochastically based semantic analysis*. Kluwer Ac., Amsterdam, The Netherlands.

Vanderveken D. 2001. Universal Grammar and Speech act Theory. *Essays in Speech Act Theory*. Eds J. Benjamin, D. Vanderveken and S. Kubo, p. 25–62.

van Noord G., Bouma G. and Koeling R. and Nederhof M. 1999. Robust grammatical analysis for spoken dialogue systems. *Natural Language Engineering*. 5(1): p. 45–93.

Zechner K. 1998. Automatic construction of frame representations for spontaneous speech in unrestricted domains. *COLING-ACL'1998. Montreal, Canada*. p. 1448–1452.

Zue V., Seneff S., Glass J., Polifrini J., Pao C., Hazen T.J. and Hetherington L. 2000. Jupiter: a telephone-based conversational interface for weather information. *IEEE Transactions on speech and audio processing*. 8(1).

An Integrated Approach to Robust Processing of Situated Spoken Dialogue

Pierre Lison
Language Technology Lab,
DFKI GmbH,
Saarbrücken, Germany
pierre.lison@dfki.de

Geert-Jan M. Kruijff
Language Technology Lab,
DFKI GmbH,
Saarbrücken, Germany
gj@dfki.de

Abstract

Spoken dialogue is notoriously hard to process with standard NLP technologies. Natural spoken dialogue is replete with disfluent, partial, elided or ungrammatical utterances, all of which are very hard to accommodate in a dialogue system. Furthermore, speech recognition is known to be a highly error-prone task, especially for complex, open-ended discourse domains. The combination of these two problems – ill-formed and/or misrecognised speech inputs – raises a major challenge to the development of robust dialogue systems.

We present an integrated approach for addressing these two issues, based on a incremental parser for Combinatory Categorial Grammar. The parser takes word lattices as input and is able to handle ill-formed and misrecognised utterances by selectively relaxing its set of grammatical rules. The choice of the most relevant interpretation is then realised via a discriminative model augmented with contextual information. The approach is fully implemented in a dialogue system for autonomous robots. Evaluation results on a Wizard of Oz test suite demonstrate very significant improvements in accuracy and robustness compared to the baseline.

1 Introduction

Spoken dialogue is often considered to be one of the most natural means of interaction between a human and a robot. It is, however, notoriously hard to process with standard language processing technologies. Dialogue utterances are often incomplete or ungrammatical, and may contain numerous disfluencies like fillers (err, uh, mm), repetitions, self-corrections, etc. Rather than getting crisp-and-clear commands such as *"Put the red ball inside the box!"*, it is more likely the robot will hear such kind of utterance: *"right, now, could you, uh, put the red ball, yeah, inside the ba/ box!"*. This is natural behaviour in human-human interaction (Fernández and Ginzburg, 2002) and can also be observed in several domain-specific corpora for human-robot interaction (Topp et al., 2006).

Moreover, even in the (rare) case where the utterance is perfectly well-formed and does not contain any kind of disfluencies, the dialogue system still needs to accomodate the various speech recognition errors thay may arise. This problem is particularly acute for robots operating in real-world noisy environments and deal with utterances pertaining to complex, open-ended domains.

The paper presents a new approach to address these two difficult issues. Our starting point is the work done by Zettlemoyer and Collins on parsing using relaxed CCG grammars (Zettlemoyer and Collins, 2007) (ZC07). In order to account for natural spoken language phenomena (more flexible word order, missing words, etc.), they augment their grammar framework with a small set of non-standard combinatory rules, leading to a *relaxation* of the grammatical constraints. A discriminative model over the parses is coupled with the parser, and is responsible for selecting the most likely interpretation(s) among the possible ones.

In this paper, we extend their approach in two important ways. First, ZC07 focused on the treatment of ill-formed input, and ignored the speech recognition issues. Our system, to the contrary, is able to deal with both ill-formed and misrecognized input, in an integrated fashion. This is done by augmenting the set of non-standard combinators with new rules specifically tailored to deal with speech recognition errors.

Second, the only features used by ZC07 are syntactic features (see 3.4 for details). We significantly extend the range of features included in the

Proceedings of EACL 2009 Workshop on Semantic Representation of Spoken Language - SRSL 2009, pages 58–65,
Athens, Greece, 30 March 2009.

discriminative model, by incorporating not only *syntactic*, but also *acoustic*, *semantic* and *contextual* information into the model.

An overview of the paper is as follows. We first describe in Section 2 the cognitive architecture in which our system has been integrated. We then discuss the approach in detail in Section 3. Finally, we present in Section 4 the quantitative evaluations on a WOZ test suite, and conclude.

2 Architecture

The approach we present in this paper is fully implemented and integrated into a cognitive architecture for autonomous robots. A recent version of this system is described in (Hawes et al., 2007). It is capable of building up visuo-spatial models of a dynamic local scene, continuously plan and execute manipulation actions on objects within that scene. The robot can discuss objects and their material- and spatial properties for the purpose of visual learning and manipulation tasks.

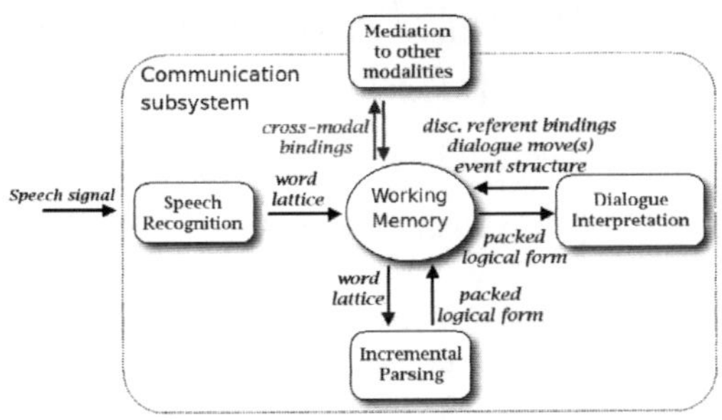

Figure 1: Architecture schema of the communication subsystem (only for comprehension).

Figure 2 illustrates the architecture schema for the communication subsystem incorporated in the cognitive architecture (only the comprehension part is shown).

Starting with ASR, we process the audio signal to establish a *word lattice* containing statistically ranked hypotheses about word sequences. Subsequently, parsing constructs grammatical analyses for the given word lattice. A grammatical analysis constructs both a syntactic analysis of the utterance, and a representation of its meaning. The analysis is based on an incremental chart parser[1] for Combinatory Categorial Grammar (Steedman and Baldridge, 2009). These meaning representations are ontologically richly sorted, relational structures, formulated in a (propositional) description logic, more precisely in the HLDS formalism (Baldridge and Kruijff, 2002). The parser compacts all meaning representations into a single *packed logical form* (Carroll and Oepen, 2005; Kruijff et al., 2007). A packed LF represents content similar across the different analyses as a single graph, using over- and underspecification of how different nodes can be connected to capture lexical and syntactic forms of ambiguity.

At the level of dialogue interpretation, a packed logical form is resolved against a SDRS-like dialogue model (Asher and Lascarides, 2003) to establish contextual co-reference and dialogue moves.

Linguistic interpretations must finally be associated with extra-linguistic knowledge about the environment – dialogue comprehension hence needs to connect with other subarchitectures like vision, spatial reasoning or planning. We realise this information binding between different modalities via a specific module, called the "binder", which is responsible for the ontology-based *mediation* accross modalities (Jacobsson et al., 2008).

2.1 Context-sensitivity

The combinatorial nature of language provides virtually unlimited ways in which we can communicate meaning. This, of course, raises the question of how precisely an utterance should then be understood as it is being heard. Empirical studies have investigated what information humans use when comprehending spoken utterances. An important observation is that interpretation *in context* plays a crucial role in the comprehension of utterance as it unfolds (Knoeferle and Crocker, 2006). During utterance comprehension, humans combine linguistic information with scene understanding and "world knowledge".

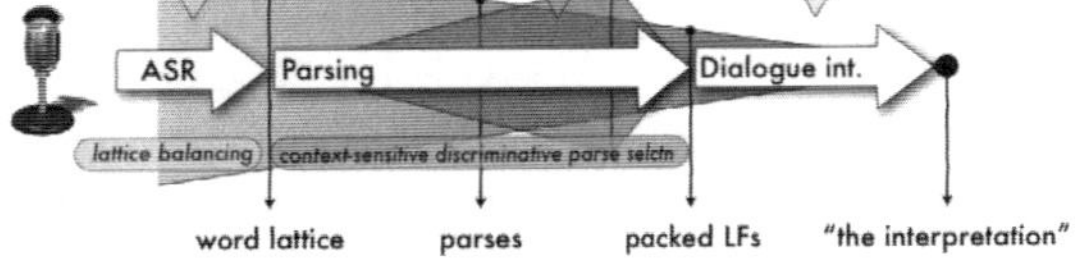

Figure 2: Context-sensitivity in processing situated dialogue understanding

Several approaches in situated dialogue for human-robot interaction have made similar obser-

[1]Built on top of the OpenCCG NLP library: http://openccg.sf.net

vations (Roy, 2005; Roy and Mukherjee, 2005; Brick and Scheutz, 2007; Kruijff et al., 2007): A robot's understanding can be improved by relating utterances to the situated context. As we will see in the next section, by incorporating contextual information into our model, our approach to robust processing of spoken dialogue seeks to exploit this important insight.

3 Approach

3.1 Grammar relaxation

Our approach to robust processing of spoken dialogue rests on the idea of **grammar relaxation**: the grammatical constraints specified in the grammar are "relaxed" to handle slightly ill-formed or misrecognised utterances.

Practically, the grammar relaxation is done via the introduction of *non-standard CCG rules* (Zettlemoyer and Collins, 2007). In Combinatory Categorial Grammar, the rules are used to assemble categories to form larger pieces of syntactic and semantic structure. The standard rules are application ($<, >$), composition (**B**), and type raising (**T**) (Steedman and Baldridge, 2009).

Several types of non-standard rules have been introduced. We describe here the two most important ones: the *discourse-level composition rules*, and the *ASR correction rules*. We invite the reader to consult (Lison, 2008) for more details on the complete set of grammar relaxation rules.

3.1.1 Discourse-level composition rules

In natural spoken dialogue, we may encounter utterances containing several independent "chunks" without any explicit separation (or only a short pause or a slight change in intonation), such as

(1) "yes take the ball no the other one on your left right and now put it in the box."

Even if retrieving a fully structured parse for this utterance is difficult to achieve, it would be useful to have access to a list of smaller "discourse units". Syntactically speaking, a discourse unit can be any type of saturated atomic categories - from a simple discourse marker to a full sentence.

The type raising rule $\mathbf{T}_{du}$ allows the conversion of atomic categories into discourse units:

$$\mathsf{A} : @_i f \Rightarrow \mathsf{du} : @_i f \qquad (\mathbf{T}_{du})$$

where A represents an arbitrary saturated atomic category (s, np, pp, etc.).

The rule $>_C$ is responsible for the integration of two discourse units into a single structure:

$$\begin{aligned} &\mathsf{du} : @_i f, \ \ \mathsf{du} : @_j g \Rightarrow \\ &\quad \mathsf{du} : @_{\{d:\text{d-units}\}}(\mathbf{list} \wedge \\ &\qquad\qquad (\langle \text{FIRST} \rangle\ i \wedge f) \wedge \\ &\qquad\qquad (\langle \text{NEXT} \rangle\ j \wedge g)) \quad (>_C) \end{aligned}$$

3.1.2 ASR error correction rules

Speech recognition is a highly error-prone task. It is however possible to partially alleviate this problem by inserting new error-correction rules (more precisely, new lexical entries) for the most frequently misrecognised words.

If we notice e.g. that the ASR system frequently substitutes the word "wrong" for the word "round" during the recognition (because of their phonological proximity), we can introduce a new lexical entry in the lexicon in order to correct this error:

$$round \vdash \mathsf{adj} : @_{attitude}(\mathbf{wrong}) \qquad (2)$$

A set of thirteen new lexical entries of this type have been added to our lexicon to account for the most frequent recognition errors.

3.2 Parse selection

Using more powerful grammar rules to relax the grammatical analysis tends to increase the number of parses. We hence need a a mechanism to discriminate among the possible parses. The task of selecting the most likely interpretation among a set of possible ones is called *parse selection*. Once all the possible parses for a given utterance are computed, they are subsequently filtered or selected in order to retain only the most likely interpretation(s). This is done via a (discriminative) statistical model covering a large number of features.

Formally, the task is defined as a function $F : \mathcal{X} \rightarrow \mathcal{Y}$ where the domain $\mathcal{X}$ is the set of possible inputs (in our case, $\mathcal{X}$ is the set of possible *word lattices*), and $\mathcal{Y}$ the set of parses. We assume:

1. A function $\mathbf{GEN}(x)$ which enumerates all possible parses for an input x. In our case, this function simply represents the set of parses of x which are admissible according to the CCG grammar.

2. A d-dimensional feature vector $\mathbf{f}(x, y) \in \Re^d$, representing specific features of the pair (x, y). It can include various acoustic, syntactic, semantic or contextual features which can be relevant in discriminating the parses.

3. A parameter vector $\mathbf{w} \in \Re^d$.

The function F, mapping a word lattice to its most likely parse, is then defined as:

$$F(x) = \underset{y \in \mathbf{GEN}(x)}{\operatorname{argmax}} \ \mathbf{w}^T \cdot \mathbf{f}(x, y) \qquad (3)$$

where $\mathbf{w}^T \cdot \mathbf{f}(x, y)$ is the inner product $\sum_{s=1}^{d} w_s \ f_s(x, y)$, and can be seen as a measure of the "quality" of the parse. Given the parameters $\mathbf{w}$, the optimal parse of a given utterance x can be therefore easily determined by enumerating all the parses generated by the grammar, extracting their features, computing the inner product $\mathbf{w}^T \cdot \mathbf{f}(x, y)$, and selecting the parse with the highest score.

The task of parse selection is an example of *structured classification problem*, which is the problem of predicting an output y from an input x, where the output y has a rich internal structure. In the specific case of parse selection, x is a word lattice, and y a logical form.

3.3 Learning

3.3.1 Training data

In order to estimate the parameters $\mathbf{w}$, we need a set of training examples. Unfortunately, no corpus of situated dialogue adapted to our task domain is available to this day, let alone semantically annotated. The collection of in-domain data via Wizard of Oz experiments being a very costly and time-consuming process, we followed the approach advocated in (Weilhammer et al., 2006) and *generated* a corpus from a hand-written task grammar.

To this end, we first collected a small set of WoZ data, totalling about a thousand utterances. This set is too small to be directly used as a corpus for statistical training, but sufficient to capture the most frequent linguistic constructions in this particular context. Based on it, we designed a domain-specific CFG grammar covering most of the utterances. Each rule is associated to a semantic HLDS representation. Weights are automatically assigned to each grammar rule by parsing our corpus, hence leading to a small *stochastic CFG grammar* augmented with semantic information.

Once the grammar is specified, it is randomly traversed a large number of times, resulting in a larger set (about 25.000) of utterances along with their semantic representations. Since we are interested in handling errors arising from speech recognition, we also need to "simulate" the most frequent recognition errors. To this end, we *synthesise* each string generated by the domain-specific CFG grammar, using a text-to-speech engine[2], feed the audio stream to the speech recogniser, and retrieve the recognition result. Via this technique, we are able to easily collect a large amount of training data[3].

3.3.2 Perceptron learning

The algorithm we use to estimate the parameters $\mathbf{w}$ using the training data is a **perceptron**. The algorithm is fully online - it visits each example in turn and updates $\mathbf{w}$ if necessary. Albeit simple, the algorithm has proven to be very efficient and accurate for the task of parse selection (Collins and Roark, 2004; Collins, 2004; Zettlemoyer and Collins, 2005; Zettlemoyer and Collins, 2007).

The pseudo-code for the online learning algorithm is detailed in [**Algorithm 1**].

It works as follows: the parameters $\mathbf{w}$ are first initialised to some arbitrary values. Then, for each pair (x_i, z_i) in the training set, the algorithm searchs for the parse y' with the highest score according to the current model. If this parse happens to match the best parse which generates z_i (which we shall denote y^*), we move to the next example. Else, we perform a simple perceptron update on the parameters:

$$\mathbf{w} = \mathbf{w} + \mathbf{f}(x_i, y^*) - \mathbf{f}(x_i, y') \qquad (4)$$

The iteration on the training set is repeated T times, or until convergence.

The most expensive step in this algorithm is the calculation of $y' = \operatorname{argmax}_{y \in \mathbf{GEN}(x_i)} \mathbf{w}^T \cdot \mathbf{f}(x_i, y)$ - this is the *decoding* problem.

It is possible to prove that, provided the training set (x_i, z_i) is separable with margin $\delta > 0$, the algorithm is assured to converge after a finite number of iterations to a model with zero training errors (Collins and Roark, 2004). See also (Collins, 2004) for convergence theorems and proofs.

3.4 Features

As we have seen, the parse selection operates by enumerating the possible parses and selecting the

---

[2]We used MARY (`http://mary.dfki.de`) for the text-to-speech engine.

[3]Because of its relatively artificial character, the quality of such training data is naturally lower than what could be obtained with a genuine corpus. But, as the experimental results will show, it remains sufficient to train the perceptron for the parse selection task, and achieve significant improvements in accuracy and robustness. In a near future, we plan to progressively replace this generated training data by a real spoken dialogue corpus adapted to our task domain.

Algorithm 1 Online perceptron learning

Require: - set of n training examples $\{(x_i, z_i) : i = 1...n\}$
- T: number of iterations over the training set
- $\texttt{GEN}(x)$: function enumerating possible parses for an input x, according to the CCG grammar.
- $\texttt{GEN}(x, z)$: function enumerating possible parses for an input x and which have semantics z, according to the CCG grammar.
- $L(y)$ maps a parse tree y to its logical form.
- Initial parameter vector $\mathbf{w}_0$

% Initialise
$\mathbf{w} \leftarrow \mathbf{w}_0$

% Loop T times on the training examples
for $t = 1...T$ **do**
  for $i = 1...n$ **do**
    % Compute best parse according to current model
    Let $y' = \text{argmax}_{y \in \mathbf{GEN}(x_i)} \mathbf{w}^T \cdot \mathbf{f}(x_i, y)$
    % If the decoded parse $\neq$ expected parse, update the parameters
    if $L(y') \neq z_i$ **then**
      % Search the best parse for utterance x_i with semantics z_i
      Let $y^* = \text{argmax}_{y \in \mathbf{GEN}(x_i, z_i)} \mathbf{w}^T \cdot \mathbf{f}(x_i, y)$
      % Update parameter vector $\mathbf{w}$
      Set $\mathbf{w} = \mathbf{w} + \mathbf{f}(x_i, y^*) - \mathbf{f}(x_i, y')$
    end if
  end for
end for
return parameter vector $\mathbf{w}$

one with the highest score according to the linear model parametrised by $\mathbf{w}$.

The accuracy of our method crucially relies on the selection of "good" features $\mathbf{f}(x, y)$ for our model - that is, features which help *discriminating* the parses. They must also be relatively cheap to compute. In our model, the features are of four types: semantic features, syntactic features, contextual features, and speech recognition features.

3.4.1 Semantic features

What are the substructures of a logical form which may be relevant to discriminate the parses? We define features on the following information sources:

1. *Nominals*: for each possible pair $\langle prop, sort \rangle$, we include a feature f_i in $\mathbf{f}(x, y)$ counting the number of nominals with ontological sort $sort$ and proposition $prop$ in the logical form.

2. *Ontological sorts*: occurrences of specific ontological sorts in the logical form.

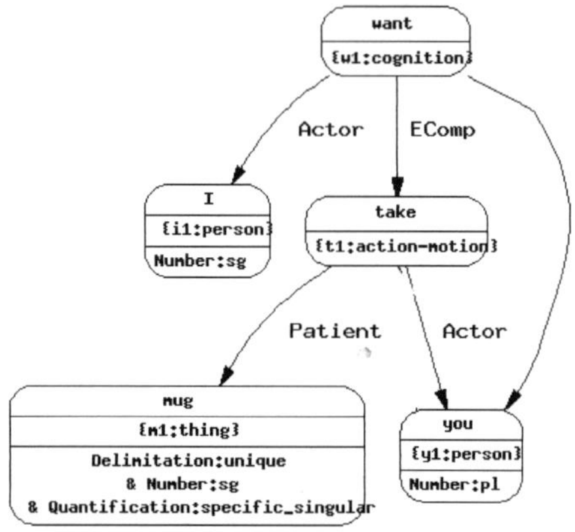

Figure 3: graphical representation of the HLDS logical form for "*I want you to take the mug*".

3. *Dependency relations*: following (Clark and Curran, 2003), we also model the *dependency structure* of the logical form. Each dependency relation is defined as a triple $\langle sort_a, sort_b, label \rangle$, where $sort_a$ denotes the sort of the incoming nominal, $sort_b$ the sort of the outgoing nominal, and $label$ is the relation label.

4. *Sequences of dependency relations*: number of occurrences of particular sequences (ie. bigram counts) of dependency relations.

The features on nominals and ontological sorts aim at modeling (aspects of) *lexical semantics* - e.g. which meanings are the most frequent for a given word -, whereas the features on relations and sequence of relations focus on *sentential semantics* - which dependencies are the most frequent. These features therefore help us handle lexical and syntactic ambiguities.

3.4.2 Syntactic features

By "syntactic features", we mean features associated to the *derivational history* of a specific parse. The main use of these features is to *penalise* to a correct extent the application of the non-standard rules introduced into the grammar.

To this end, we include in the feature vector $\mathbf{f}(x, y)$ a new feature for each non-standard rule, which counts the number of times the rule was applied in the parse.

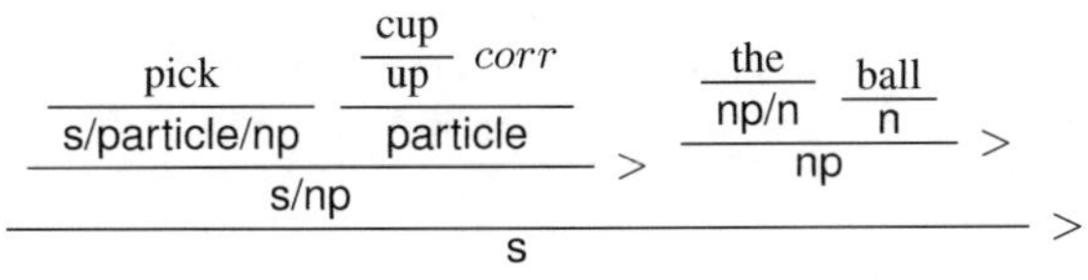

Figure 4: CCG derivation of *"pick cup the ball"*.

In the derivation shown in the figure 4, the rule *corr* (correction of a speech recognition error) is applied once, so the corresponding feature value is set to 1. The feature values for the remaining rules are set to 0, since they are absent from the parse.

These syntactic features can be seen as a *penalty* given to the parses using these non-standard rules, thereby giving a preference to the "normal" parses over them. This mechanism ensures that the grammar relaxation is only applied "as a last resort" when the usual grammatical analysis fails to provide a full parse. Of course, depending on the relative frequency of occurrence of these rules in the training corpus, some of them will be more strongly penalised than others.

3.4.3 Contextual features

As we have already outlined in the background section, one striking characteristic of spoken dialogue is the importance of *context*. Understanding the visual and discourse contexts is crucial to resolve potential ambiguities and compute the most likely interpretation(s) of a given utterance.

The feature vector $\mathbf{f}(x, y)$ therefore includes various features related to the context:

1. *Activated words*: our dialogue system maintains in its working memory a list of contextually activated words (cfr. (Lison and Kruijff, 2008)). This list is continuously updated as the dialogue and the environment evolves. For each context-dependent word, we include one feature counting the number of times it appears in the utterance string.

2. *Expected dialogue moves*: for each possible dialogue move, we include one feature indicating if the dialogue move is consistent with the current discourse model. These features ensure for instance that the dialogue move following a QuestionYN is a Accept, Reject or another question (e.g. for clarification requests), but almost never an Opening.

3. *Expected syntactic categories*: for each atomic syntactic category in the CCG grammar, we include one feature indicating if the category is consistent with the current discourse model. These features can be used to handle *sentence fragments*.

3.4.4 Speech recognition features

Finally, the feature vector $\mathbf{f}(x, y)$ also includes features related to the *speech recognition*. The ASR module outputs a set of (partial) recognition hypotheses, packed in a word lattice. One example of such a structure is given in Figure 5. Each recognition hypothesis is provided with an associated confidence score, and we want to favour the hypotheses with high confidence scores, which are, according to the statistical models incorporated in the ASR, more likely to reflect what was uttered.

To this end, we introduce three features: the *acoustic confidence score* (confidence score provided by the statistical models included in the ASR), the *semantic confidence score* (based on a "concept model" also provided by the ASR), and the *ASR ranking* (hypothesis rank in the word lattice, from best to worst).

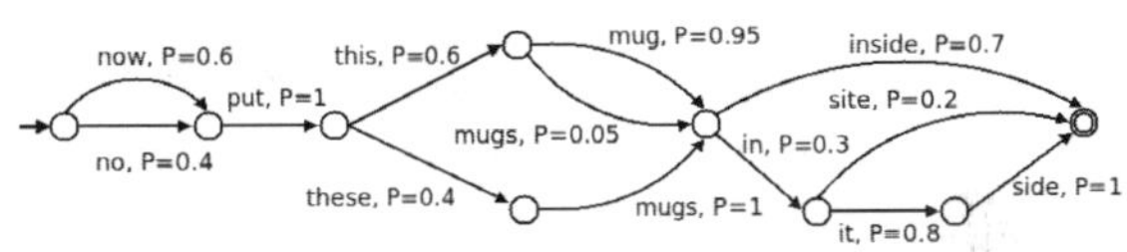

Figure 5: Example of word lattice

4 Experimental evaluation

We performed a quantitative evaluation of our approach, using its implementation in a fully integrated system (cf. Section 2). To set up the experiments for the evaluation, we have gathered a corpus of human-robot spoken dialogue for our task-domain, which we segmented and annotated manually with their expected semantic interpretation. The data set contains 195 individual utterances along with their complete logical forms.

4.1 Results

Three types of quantitative results are extracted from the evaluation results: *exact-match*, *partial-match*, and *word error rate*. Tables 1, 2 and 3 illustrate the results, broken down by use of grammar relaxation, use of parse selection, and number of recognition hypotheses considered.

	Size of word lattice (number of NBests)	Grammar relaxation	Parse selection	Precision	Recall	F_1-value
(Baseline)	1	No	No	40.9	45.2	**43.0**
.	1	No	Yes	59.0	54.3	56.6
.	1	Yes	Yes	52.7	70.8	60.4
.	3	Yes	Yes	55.3	82.9	66.3
.	5	Yes	Yes	55.6	84.0	66.9
(Full approach)	10	Yes	Yes	55.6	84.9	**67.2**

Table 1: Exact-match accuracy results (in percents).

	Size of word lattice (number of NBests)	Grammar relaxation	Parse selection	Precision	Recall	F_1-value
(Baseline)	1	No	No	86.2	56.2	**68.0**
.	1	No	Yes	87.4	56.6	68.7
.	1	Yes	Yes	88.1	76.2	81.7
.	3	Yes	Yes	87.6	85.2	86.4
.	5	Yes	Yes	87.6	86.0	86.8
(Full approach)	10	Yes	Yes	87.7	87.0	**87.3**

Table 2: Partial-match accuracy results (in percents).

Each line in the tables corresponds to a possible configuration. Tables 1 and 2 give the precision, recall and F_1 value for each configuration (respectively for the exact- and partial-match), and Table 3 gives the Word Error Rate [WER].

The first line corresponds to the baseline: no grammar relaxation, no parse selection, and use of the first NBest recognition hypothesis. The last line corresponds to the results with the full approach: grammar relaxation, parse selection, and use of 10 recognition hypotheses.

Size of word lattice (NBests)	Grammar relaxation	Parse selection	WER
1	No	No	**20.5**
1	Yes	Yes	19.4
3	Yes	Yes	16.5
5	Yes	Yes	15.7
10	Yes	Yes	**15.7**

Table 3: Word error rate (in percents).

4.2 Comparison with baseline

Here are the comparative results we obtained:

- Regarding the exact-match results between the baseline and our approach (grammar relaxation and parse selection with all features activated for NBest 10), the F_1-measure climbs from 43.0 % to 67.2 %, which means a relative difference of $\mathbf{56.3}$ %.
- For the partial-match, the F_1-measure goes from 68.0 % for the baseline to 87.3 % for our approach – a relative increase of $\mathbf{28.4}$ %.
- We obverse a significant decrease in WER: we go from 20.5 % for the baseline to 15.7 % with our approach. The difference is statistically significant (p-value for t-tests is 0.036), and the relative decrease of $\mathbf{23.4}$ %.

5 Conclusions

We presented an *integrated* approach to the processing of (situated) spoken dialogue, suited to the specific needs and challenges encountered in human-robot interaction.

In order to handle disfluent, partial, ill-formed or misrecognized utterances, the grammar used by the parser is "relaxed" via the introduction of a set of *non-standard combinators* which allow for the insertion/deletion of specific words, the combination of discourse fragments or the correction of speech recognition errors.

The relaxed parser yields a (potentially large) set of parses, which are then packed and retrieved by the parse selection module. The parse selection is based on a discriminative model exploring a set of relevant semantic, syntactic, contextual and acoustic features extracted for each parse. The parameters of this model are estimated against an automatically generated corpus of $\langle$utterance, logical form$\rangle$ pairs. The learning algorithm is an perceptron, a simple albeit efficient technique for parameter estimation.

As forthcoming work, we shall examine the potential extension of our approach in new directions, such as the exploitation of parse selection for *incremental* scoring/pruning of the parse chart, the introduction of more refined contextual features, or the use of more sophisticated learning algorithms, such as Support Vector Machines.

References

Nicholas Asher and Alex Lascarides. 2003. *Logics of Conversation*. Cambridge University Press.

J. Baldridge and G.-J. M. Kruijff. 2002. Coupling CCG and hybrid logic dependency semantics. In *ACL'02: Proceedings of the 40th Annual Meeting of the Association for Computational Linguistics*, pages 319–326, Philadelphia, PA. Association for Computational Linguistics.

T. Brick and M. Scheutz. 2007. Incremental natural language processing for HRI. In *Proceeding of the ACM/IEEE international conference on Human-Robot Interaction (HRI'07)*, pages 263 – 270.

J. Carroll and S. Oepen. 2005. High efficiency realization for a wide-coverage unification grammar. In *Proceedings of the International Joint Conference on Natural Language Processing (IJCNLP'05)*, pages 165–176.

Stephen Clark and James R. Curran. 2003. Log-linear models for wide-coverage ccg parsing. In *Proceedings of the 2003 conference on Empirical methods in natural language processing*, pages 97–104, Morristown, NJ, USA. Association for Computational Linguistics.

Michael Collins and Brian Roark. 2004. Incremental parsing with the perceptron algorithm. In *ACL '04: Proceedings of the 42nd Annual Meeting of the Association for Computational Linguistics*, page 111, Morristown, NJ, USA. Association for Computational Linguistics.

Michael Collins. 2004. Parameter estimation for statistical parsing models: theory and practice of distribution-free methods. In *New developments in parsing technology*, pages 19–55. Kluwer Academic Publishers.

R. Fernández and J. Ginzburg. 2002. A corpus study of non-sentential utterances in dialogue. *Traitement Automatique des Langues*, 43(2):12–43.

N. Hawes, A. Sloman, J. Wyatt, M. Zillich, H. Jacobsson, G.J. M. Kruijff, M. Brenner, G. Berginc, and D. Skocaj. 2007. Towards an integrated robot with multiple cognitive functions. In *AAAI*, pages 1548–1553. AAAI Press.

Henrik Jacobsson, Nick Hawes, Geert-Jan Kruijff, and Jeremy Wyatt. 2008. Crossmodal content binding in information-processing architectures. In *Proceedings of the 3rd ACM/IEEE International Conference on Human-Robot Interaction (HRI)*, Amsterdam, The Netherlands, March 12–15.

P. Knoeferle and M.C. Crocker. 2006. The coordinated interplay of scene, utterance, and world knowledge: evidence from eye tracking. *Cognitive Science*.

G.J.M. Kruijff, P. Lison, T. Benjamin, H. Jacobsson, and N.A. Hawes. 2007. Incremental, multi-level processing for comprehending situated dialogue in human-robot interaction. In *Language and Robots: Proceedings from the Symposium (LangRo'2007)*, pages 55–64, Aveiro, Portugal, December.

Pierre Lison and Geert-Jan M. Kruijff. 2008. Salience-driven contextual priming of speech recognition for human-robot interaction. In *Proceedings of the 18th European Conference on Artificial Intelligence*, Patras (Greece).

Pierre Lison. 2008. Robust processing of situated spoken dialogue. Master's thesis, Universität des Saarlandes, Saarbrücken.

D. Roy and N. Mukherjee. 2005. Towards situated speech understanding: visual context priming of language models. *Computer Speech & Language*, 19(2):227–248, April.

D.K. Roy. 2005. Semiotic schemas: A framework for grounding language in action and perception. *Artificial Intelligence*, 167(1-2):170–205.

Mark Steedman and Jason Baldridge. 2009. Combinatory categorial grammar. In Robert Borsley and Kersti Börjars, editors, *Nontransformational Syntax: A Guide to Current Models*. Blackwell, Oxford.

E. A. Topp, H. Hüttenrauch, H.I. Christensen, and K. Severinson Eklundh. 2006. Bringing together human and robotic environment representations – a pilot study. In *Proc. of the IEEE/RSJ International Conference on Intelligent Robots and Systems (IROS)*, Beijing, China, October.

Karl Weilhammer, Matthew N. Stuttle, and Steve Young. 2006. Bootstrapping language models for dialogue systems. In *Proceedings of INTERSPEECH 2006*, Pittsburgh, PA.

Luke S. Zettlemoyer and Michael Collins. 2005. Learning to map sentences to logical form: Structured classification with probabilistic categorial grammars. In *UAI '05, Proceedings of the 21st Conference in Uncertainty in Artificial Intelligence, July 2005*, pages 658–666.

Luke Zettlemoyer and Michael Collins. 2007. Online learning of relaxed CCG grammars for parsing to logical form. In *Proceedings of the 2007 Joint Conference on Empirical Methods in Natural Language Processing and Computational Natural Language Learning (EMNLP-CoNLL)*, pages 678–687.

RUBISC - a Robust Unification-Based Incremental Semantic Chunker

Michaela Atterer
Department for Linguistics
University of Potsdam
atterer@ling.uni-potsdam.de

David Schlangen
Department for Linguistics
University of Potsdam
das@ling.uni-potsdam.de

Abstract

We present RUBISC, a new incremental chunker that can perform incremental slot filling and revising as it receives a stream of words. Slot values can influence each other via a unification mechanism. Chunks correspond to sense units, and end-of-sentence detection is done incrementally based on a notion of semantic/pragmatic completeness. One of RUBISC's main fields of application is in dialogue systems where it can contribute to responsiveness and hence naturalness, because it can provide a partial or complete semantics of an utterance while the speaker is still speaking. The chunker is evaluated on a German transcribed speech corpus and achieves a concept error rate of 43.3% and an F-Score of 81.5.

1 Introduction

Real-time NLP applications such as dialogue systems can profit considerably from incremental processing of language. When syntactic and semantic structure is built on-line while the speech recognition (ASR) is still working on the speech stream, unnatural silences can be avoided and the system can react in a faster and more user-friendly way. As (Aist et al., 2007) and (Skantze and Schlangen, 2009) show, such incremental systems are typically preferred by users over non-incremental systems.

To achieve incrementality, most dialogue systems employ an incremental chart parser (cf. (Stoness et al., 2004; Seginer, 2007) etc.). However, most existing dialogue systems operate in very limited domains, e.g. moving objects, people, trains etc. from one place to another (cf. (Aist et al., 2007), (Skantze, 2007), (Traum et al., 1996)). The complexity of the semantic representations needed is thus limited. Moreover, user behaviour (ungrammatical sentences, hesitations, false starts) and error-prone ASR require the parsing process to be robust.[1] We argue that obtaining relatively flat semantics in a limited domain while needing exigent robustness calls for investigating shallower incremental chunking approaches as alternatives to CFG or dependency parsing. Previous work that uses a combination of shallow and deep parsing in dialogue systems also indicates that shallow methods can be superior to deep parsing (Lewin et al., 1999).

The question addressed in this paper is how to construct a chunker that works incrementally and robustly and builds the semantics required in a dialogue system. In our framework chunks are built according to the semantic information they contain while syntactic structure itself is less important. This approach is inspired by Selkirk's sense units (Selkirk, 1984). She claims such units to be relevant for prosodic structure and different to syntactic structure. Similarly, (Abney, 1991) describes some characteristics of chunks as follows—properties which also make them seem to be useful units to be considered in spoken dialogue systems:

"when I read a sentence, I read it a chunk at a time. [...] These chunks correspond in some way to prosodic patterns. Chunks also represent a grammatical watershed of sorts. The typical chunk consists of a single content word surrounded by a constellation of function words, matching a fixed template. By contrast, the relationships between chunks are mediated more by lexical selection

[1] cf. The incremental parser in (Skantze, 2007) can jump over a configurable number of words in the input.

Proceedings of EACL 2009 Workshop on Semantic Representation of Spoken Language - SRSL 2009, pages 66–73,
Athens, Greece, 30 March 2009. ©2009 Association for Computational Linguistics

than by rigid templates. [...] and the order in which chunks occur is much more flexible than the order of words within chunks."

In our approach chunks are built incrementally (one at a time) and are defined semantically (a sense unit is complete when a slot in our template or frame semantics can be filled). Ideally, in a full system, the definition of their boundaries will also be aided by prosodic information. The current implementation builds the chunks or sense units by identifying a more or less fixed sequence of content and function words, similar to what Abney describes as a fixed template. The relationships between the units are mediated by a unification mechanism which prevents selectional restrictions from being violated. This allows the order of the sense units to be flexible, even as flexible as they appear in ungrammatical utterances. This unification mechanism and the incremental method of operation are also the main difference to Abney's work and other chunkers.

In this paper, we first present our approach of chunking, show our grammar formalism, the main features of the chunker (unification mechanism, incrementality, robustness), and explain how the chunker can cope with certain tasks that are an issue in dialogue systems, such as online utterance endpointing and revising hypotheses. In Section 3, we evaluate the chunker on a German corpus (of transcribed spontaneous speech) in terms of concept error rate and slot filling accuracy. Then we discuss related work, followed by a general discussion and the conclusion.

2 Incremental Chunking

Figure 1 shows a simple example where the chunker segments the input stream incrementally into semantically relevant chunks. The figure also displays how the frame is being filled incrementally. The chunk grammar developed for this work and the dialogue corpus used were German, but we give some examples in English for better readability.

As time passes the chunker receives more and more words from the ASR. It puts the words in a queue and waits until the semantic content of the accumulated words is enough for filling a slot in the frame semantics. When this is the case the chunk is completed and a new chunk is started. At the same time the frame semantics is updated if slot unification (see below) is possible and a check

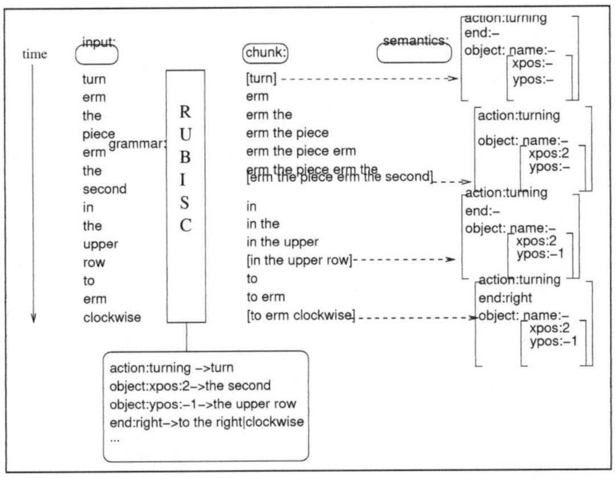

Figure 1: Incremental robust sense unit construction by RUBISC.

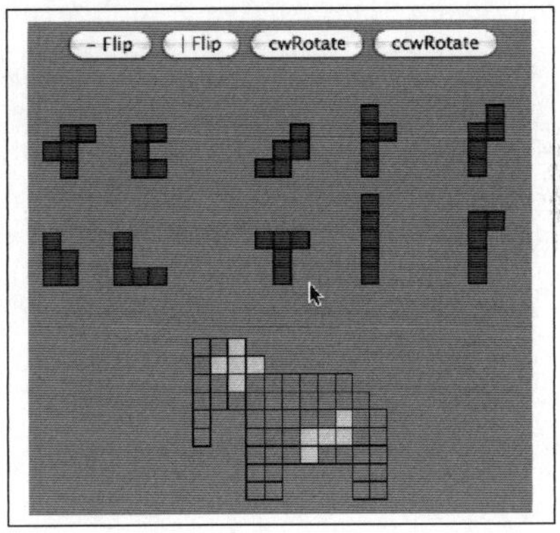

Figure 2: Puzzle-task of the corpus used for grammar building and testing.

whether the utterance is complete is made, so that the chunker can be restarted for the next utterance if necessary.

2.1 A Regular Grammar for Semantics

The grammar we are using for the experiments in this paper was developed using a small corpus of German dialogue (Siebert and Schlangen, 2008), (Siebert, 2007). Figure 2 shows a picture of the task that the subjects completed for this corpus.[2] A number of pentomino pieces were presented. The pieces had to be moved into an animal-shaped figure. The subjects were shown partly completed puzzles and had to give concise and detailed verbal instructions of the next move that had to be done. The locations inside this figure were usually referred to in terms of body parts (*move the x into*

[2]For the corpus used here the difference was that the button labels were German and that the pentomino pieces were not ordered in two rows. For better readability, we show the picture with the English labels.

the head of the elephant).

For such restricted tasks, a simple frame semantics seems sufficient, representing the action (grasping, movement, flipping or turning of an object), the object that is involved, and where or in which position the object will end up. In our current grammar implementation the object can be described with three attributes: `name` is the name of the object. In our domain, the objects are pentomino-pieces (i.e., geometrical forms that can be built out of five squares) which have traditional letter names such as `x` or `w`; the grammar maps other descriptions such as *cross* or *plus* to such canonical names. A piece can also be described by its current position, as in *the lower piece in the third column*. This is covered by the attributes `xpos` and `ypos` demarking the x-position and y-position of a piece. The x- or y-position can be a positive or negative number, depending on whether the description counts from left or right, respectively.

The possible slots must be defined in the grammar file in the following format:

```
@:action
@:entity:name
@:entity:xpos
@:entity:ypos
@:end
```

(That is: `definition marker @:level 1: (optional) level 2.`)

The position where or in which the piece ends up could also be coded as a complex entry, but for simplicity's sake (in the data used for evaluation, we have a very limited set of end positions that would each be described by just one attribute respectively), we restrict ourselves to a simple entry called `end` which takes the value of a body part (*head, back, leg1* etc.) in the case of movement, and the value of a direction or end position *horizontal, vertical, right, left* in the case of a turning or flipping action. It will be (according to our current grammar) set to *empty* in the case of a grasping action, because grasping does not specify an end position. This will also become important later, when unification comes into play. Figure 3 shows a part of the German grammar used with approximate translations (in curly brackets) of the right-hand side into English. The English parts in curly brackets is meta-notation and not part of the grammar file. Note that one surface string can determine the value of more than one semantic slot. The grammar used in the experiments in this paper had 97 rules.

```
action:grasping,end:empty -> nimm|nehme
                                              {take}
action:turning   -> drehe?           {turn}
action:flipping  -> spieg(le|el)     {flip}
action:movement  -> bewegt           {moved}
action:turning   -> gedreht          {turned}
entity:name:x -> kreuz|plus|((das|ein) x)
                            {cross|pluss|((the|an) x)}
entity:name:w -> treppe|((das|ein) w$)
                                 {staircase|(the|a) w}
entity:name:w -> (das|ein) m$
                                      {(the|an) m}
entity:name:z -> (das|ein) z$
                                       {(the|a) z}
end:head        -> (in|an) den kopf
                                   {(on|in) the head}
end:leg2 -> ins? das (hinterbein|hintere
  bein|rechte bein|zweites bein) {in the hindleg|
                        back leg|right leg| second leg}
entity:ypos:lower -> der (unteren|zweiten)
                         reihe {(lower|second) row}
entity:xpos:1  -> das erste       {the first}
entity:ypos:-1 -> das letzte      {the last}
end:horizontal,action:flipping -> horizontal
                                      {horizontally}
```

Figure 3: Fragment of the grammar file used in the experiments (with English translations of the patterns for illustration only).

2.2 Unification

Unification is an important feature of RUBISC for handling aspects of long-distance dependencies and preventing wrong semantic representations. Unification enables a form of 'semantic specification' of verb arguments, avoiding that the wrong arguments are combined with a given verb. It also makes possible that rules can check for the value of other slots and hence possibly become inapplicable. The verb *move*, for instance, ensures that `action` is set to *movement*. For the utterance *schieb das äh das horizontal äh liegt ins Vorderbein* (*move that uh which is horizontal into the front leg*). The `action`-slot will be filled with *movement* but the `end`-slot remains empty because *horizontal* as an end fits only with a flipping action, and so is ignored here. Figure 4 illustrates how the slot unification mechanism works.

2.3 Robustness

The chunker meets various robustness requirements to a high degree. First, pronunciation variants can be taken account of in the grammar in a very flexible way, because the surface string or terminal symbols can be expressed through regu-

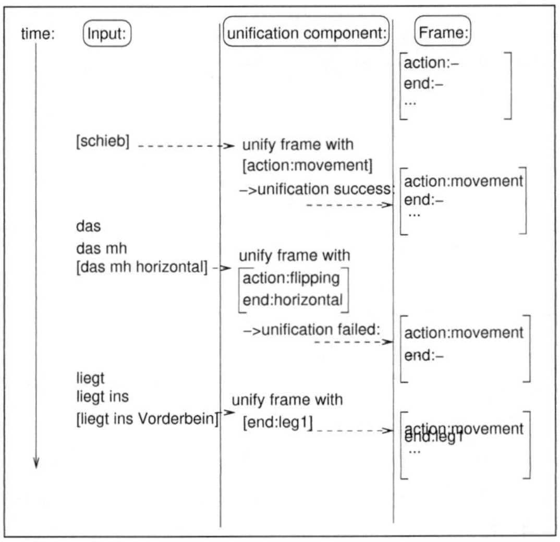

Figure 4: Example of slot unification and failure of unification.

lar expression patterns. *move* in German for instance can be pronounced with or without a final *-e* as *bewege* or *beweg*. *flip* (*spiegle* can be pronounced with or without *-el*-inversion at the end. Note, that this is due to the performance of speakers in our corpus and does not necessarily reflect German grammar rules. A system, however, needs to be able to cope with performance-based variations.

Disfluencies are handled through how the chunker constructs chunks as sense units. First, the chunker only searches for relevant information in a chunk. Irrelevant information such as an initial *uh* in *uh second row* is put in the queue, but ignored as the chunker picks only *second row* as the semantically relevant part. Furthermore the chunker provides a mechanism that allows it to jump over words, so that *second row* will be found in *the second uh row* and *the cross* will be found in *the strange cross*, where *strange* is an unknown word.

2.4 Incrementality

One of the main features of RUBISC is its incrementality. It can receive one word at a time and extract semantic structure from it. Incrementality is not strict here in the sense of (Nivre, 2004), because sometimes more than one word is needed before parts of the frame are constructed and output: *into the right*, for instance, needs to wait for a word like *leg* that completes the chunk. We don't necessarily consider this a disadvantage, though, as our chunks closely correlate to the minimal bits of information that can usefully be reacted to. In our corpus the first slot gets on average filled after 3.5 words (disregarding examples where no slots are filled). The average utterance is 12.4 words long.

2.5 End-of-Sentence Detection

An incremental parser in a dialogue system needs to know when to stop processing a sentence and when to start the next one. This can be done by using prosodic and syntactic information (Atterer et al., 2008) or by checking whether a syntactic S-node is complete. Since RUBISC builds sense units, the completeness of an utterance can be defined as semantic-pragmatic completeness, i.e. by a certain number of slots that must be filled. In our domain, for instance, it makes sense to restart the chunker when the action and end slot and either the name slot or the two position slots are filled.

2.6 History

The chunker keeps a history of the states of the frames. It is able to go back to a previous state when the incremental speech recognition revokes a word hypothesis. As an example consider the current word hypothesis to be *the L*. The slot entity name will be filled with *l*. Then the speech recognition decides to change the hypothesis into *the elephant*. This results in clearing the slot for entity name again.

3 Evaluation

The sense unit chunker was evaluated in terms of how well it performed in slot filling on an unseen part of our corpus. This corpus comes annotated with utterance boundaries. 500 of these utterances were manually labelled in terms of the semantic slots defined in the grammar. The annotators were not involved in the construction of the chunker or grammar. The annotation guidelines detailed the possible values for each slot. The entity names had to be filled in with the letter names of the pieces, the end slot with body parts or *right, left, horizontal* etc., and the position slots with positive and negative numbers.[3] The chunker was then run on 400 of these utterances and the slot values were compared with the annotated frames. 100 of the labelled utterances and 50 additional utter-

[3]In a small fraction (21) of the 500 cases an utterance actually contained 2 statements that were combined with *und/and*. In these cases the second statement was neglected.

ances were used by the author for developing the grammar.

We examined the following evaluation measures:

- the concept error (**concept err**) rate (percentage of wrong frames)
- the percentage of complete frames that were correct (**frames corr**)
- the percentage of **slots** that were **corr**ect
- the percentage of **action** slots **corr**ect
- the percentage of **end** slots **corr**ect
- the percentage of object:**name** slots **corr**ect
- the percentage of object:**xpos** slots **corr**ect
- the percentage of object:**ypos** slots **corr**ect

The results are shown in Table 1. We used a very simple baseline: a system that does not fill any slots. This strategy still gets 17% of the frames right, because some utterances do not contain any real content. For the sentence *Also das ist recht schwer* (Trans: *That's quite difficult.*), for instance, the gold standard semantic representation would be: `{action:None, end:None, object:{xpos:None, name:None, ypos:None}}`. As the baseline 'system' always returns the empty frame, it scores perfectly for this example sentence. We are aware that this appears to be a very easy baseline. However, for some slots, such as the xpos and ypos slots it still turned out to be quite hard to beat this baseline, as wrong entries were common for those slots. The chunker achieves a frame accuracy of 54.5% and an overall slot filling accuracy of 86.80% (compared to 17% and 64.3% baseline). Of the individual slots the action slot was the one that improved the most. The position slots were the only ones to deteriorate. As 17% of our utterances did not contain any relevant content, i.e. the frame was completely empty, we repeated the evaluation without these irrelevant data. The results are shown in brackets in the table.

To check the impact of the unification mechanism, we performed another evaluation with this mechanism turned off, i.e. slots are always filled when they are empty without regarding other slots. In the second step in Figure 4, the end slot would hence be filled. This resulted in a decline in performance as can also be seen in Table 1. We also turned off robustness features to test for their impact. Surprisingly, turning off the skipping of one word within a string specified by a grammar rule (as in *to erm clockwise*), did not have an effect on the results on our corpus. When we also turn off allowing initial material (*erm the piece*), however, performance drops considerably.

We also tested a variant of the system *RUBISC-o* (for *RUBISC-overlap*) which considers overlapping chunks: *Take the third piece* will result in `xpos:3` for the original chunker, even if the utterance is continued with *from the right*. *RUBISC-o* also considers the previous chunk *the third piece* for the search of a surface representation. In this case, it overwrites `3` with `-3`. In general, this behaviour improves the results.[4]

To allow a comparison with other work that reports recall and precision as measures, we also computed those values for RUBISC: for our test corpus recall was 83.47% and precision was 79.69% (F-score 81.54). A direct comparison with other systems is of course not possible, because the tasks and data are different. Nevertheless, the numbers allow an approximate feel of how well the system performs.

To get an even better idea of the performance, we let a second annotator label the data we tested on; inter-annotator agreement is given in Table 1. The accuracy for most slots is around 90% agreement beween annotators. The concept error rate is 32.25%. We also examined 50 utterances of the test corpus for an error analysis. The largest part of the errors was due to vocabulary restrictions or restrictions in the regular expressions: subjects used names for pieces or body parts or even verbs which had not been seen or considered during grammar development. As our rules for end positions contained pronouns like (*into the back*), they were too restricted for some description variants (*such that it touches the back*). Another problem that appears is that descriptions of starting positions can be confounded with descriptions of end positions. Sometimes subjects refer to end positions not with body parts but with *at the right side* etc. In some cases this leads to wrong entries in the object-position slots. In some cases a full parser might be helpful, but not always, because some expressions are syntactically ambiguous: *füge das Teil ganz rechts in das Rechteck ein.* (*put the piece on the right into the square/put the piece into the square on the right.*) A minority of errors was also

[4]Testing significance, there is a significant difference between RUBISC and the baseline, and RUBISC and RIBISC *w/o rob* (for all measures except *xpos* and *ypos*). The other variants show no significance compared with RUBISC but clear tendencies in the directions described above.

	baseline	RUBISC	w/o unif	w/o rob	RUBISC-o	i-annotator
concept err	83.0 (100)	45.5 (44.6)	49.5 (49.7)	73.3 (85.5)	43.3 (42.8)	32.3 (35.5)
frames corr	17.0 (0)	54.5 (55.4)	50.3 (50.3)	26.8 (14.5)	56.8 (57.2)	67.8 (64.5)
slots corr	64.3 (57.0)	86.8 (87.2)	84.6 (84.5)	78.8 (74.9)	87.6 (87.6)	92.1 (91.5)
action corr	27.8 (13.0)	90.3 (92.2)	85.8 (86.7)	64.3 (57.5)	89.8 (90.7)	89.0 (88.6)
end corr	68.0 (61.4)	85.8 (87.3)	81.0 (81.6)	73.8 (69.0)	85.5 (87.0)	95.8 (95.1)
name corr	48.8 (38.3)	86.3 (88.3)	84.5 (86.1)	79.0 (76.2)	86.5 (88.0)	86.8 (85.8)
xpos corr	87.5 (84.9)	83.0 (80.7)	83.0 (80.7)	86.5 (83.7)	85.5 (83.4)	94.5 (94.0)
ypos corr	89.5 (87.3)	88.8 (87.3)	88.8 (87.3)	90.3 (88.3)	90.5 (88.9)	94.5 (94.0)

Table 1: Evaluation results (in %) for RUBISC in comparison with the baseline, RUBISC without unification mechanism (w/o unif), without robustness (w/o rob), RUBISC with overlap (RUBISC-o), and inter-annotator aggreement (i-annotator). See the text for more information.

due to complex descriptions (*the damaged t where the right part has dropped downwards* – referring to the f), transcription errors (*recht* statt *rechts*) etc.

4 Related Work

Slot filling is used in dialogue systems such as the Ravenclaw-Olympus system[5], but the slots are filled by using output from a chart parser (Ward, 2008). The idea is similar in that word strings are mapped onto semantic frames. A filled slot, however, does not influence other slots via unification as in our framework, nor can the system deal with incrementality. This is also the main difference to systems such as Regulus (Rayner et al., 2006). Our unification is carried out on filled slots and in an incremental fashion. It is not directly specified in our grammar formalism. The chunker rather checks whether slot entries suggested by various independent grammar rules are unifiable.

Even though not incremental either, the approach by (Milward, 2000) is similar in that it can pick information from various parts of an utterance; for example, it can extract the arrival time from sentences like *I'd like to arrive at York now let's see yes at 3pm*. It builds a semantic chart using a Categorial grammar. The entries of this chart are then mapped into slots. A number of settings are compared and evaluated using recall and precision measures. The setting with the highest recall (52%) achieves a precision of 79%. The setting with the highest precision (96%) a recall of 22%. These are F-scores of 62.7 and 35.8 respectively.

(Aist, 2006) incrementally identifies what they call 'pragmatic fragments', which resemble the sense units produced in this paper. However, their system is provided with syntactic labels and the idea is to pass those on to a parser (this part appears to not be implemented yet). No evaluation is given.

(Zechner, 1998) also builds frame representations. Contrary to our approach, semantic information is extracted in a second step after syntactic chunks have been defined. The approach does not address the issue of end of sentence-detection, and also differs in that it was designed for use with unrestricted domains and hence requires resources such as WordNet (Miller et al., 1993). Depending on the WordNet output, usually more than one frame representation is built. In an evaluation, in 21.4% of the cases one of the frames found is correct. Other approaches like (Rose, 2000) also need lexicons or similar resources.

(Helbig and Hartrumpf, 1997) developed an incremental word-oriented parser for German that uses the notion of semantic kernels. This idea is similar in that increments correspond to constituents that have already been understood semantically. The parser was later on mainly used for question answering systems and, even though strongly semantically oriented, places more emphasis on syntactic and morphological analysis and less on robustness than our approach. It uses quite complex representations in the form of multi-layered extended semantic networks.

Finally, speech grammars such as JSFG[6] are similar in that recognition patterns for slots like 'action' are defined via regular patterns. The main differences are non-incrementality and that the result of employing the grammar is a legal sequential string for each individual slot, while our grammar

[5] `http://www.ravenclaw-olympus.org/`

[6] `java.sun.com/products/java-media/speech/forDevelopers/JSGF/`

also encodes, what is a legal (distributed) combination of slot entries.

5 Discussion and Future Work

The RUBISC chunker presented here is not the first NLU component that is robust against unknown words or structures, or non-grammaticalities and disfluencies in the input, nor the first that works incrementally, or chunk-based, or focusses predominantly on semantic content instead of syntactic structure. But we believe that it is the first that is all of this combined, and that the combination of these features provides an advantage—at least for the domains that we are working on. The novel combination of unification and incrementality has the potential to handle more phenomena than simple key word spotting. Consider the sentence: *Do not take the piece that looks like an* s*, rather the one that looks like a* w. The idea is to introduce a negation slot or flag, that will be set when a negation occurs. *nicht das s* (not the s) will trigger the flag to be set while at the same time the name slot is filled with s. This negation slot could then trigger a switch of the mode of integration of new semantic information from unification to overwriting. We will test this in future work.

One of the main restrictions of our approach is that the grammar is strongly word-oriented and does not abstract over syntactic categories. Its expressive power is thus limited and some extra coding work might be necessary due to the lack of generalization. However, we feel that this is mediated by the simplicity of the grammar formalism. A grammar for a restricted domain (and the approach is mainly aiming at such domains) like ours can be developed within a short time and its limited size also restricts the extra coding work. Another possible objection to our approach is that handcrafting grammars like ours is costly and to some extent arbitrary. However, for a small specialized vocabulary as is typical for many dialogue systems, we believe that our approach can lead to a good fast-running system in a short developing time due to the simplicity of the grammar formalism and algorithm, which makes it easier to handle than systems that use large lexical resources for complexer domains (e.g. tutoring systems). Other future directions are to expand the unification mechanism and grammar formalism such that alternatives for slots are possible. This feature would allow the grammar writer to specify that end:right requires a turning action *or* a flipping action.

6 Conclusion

We presented a novel framework for chunking. The main new ideas are that of incremental chunking and chunking by sense units, where the relationship between chunks is established via a unification mechanism instead of syntactic bounds, as in a full parsing approach. This mechanism is shown to have advantages over simple keyword spotting. The approach is suitable for online end-of-sentence detection and can handle revised word hypotheses. It is thus suitable for use in a spoken dialogue system which aims at incrementality and responsiveness. Nevertheless it can also be used for other NLP applications. It can be used in an incremental setting, but also for non-incremental tasks. The grammar format is easy to grasp, and the user can specify the slots he wants to be filled. In an evaluation it achieved a concept error rate of 43.25% compared to a simple baseline of 83%.

7 Acknowledgement

This work was funded by the DFG Emmy-Noether grant SCHL845/3-1. Many thanks to Ewan Klein for valuable comments. All errors are of course ours.

References

Steven Abney. 1991. Parsing by chunks. In *Principle-based Parsing: Computation and Psycholinguistics*, volume 44 of *Studies in Linguistics and Philosophy*. Kluwer.

Gregory Aist, James Allen, Ellen Campana, Carlos Gomez Gallo, Scott Stoness, Mary Swift, and Michael K. Tanenhaus. 2007. Incremental understanding in human-computer dialogue and experimental evidence for advantages over nonincremental methods. In *Decalog 2007*, Trento, Italy.

Gregory S. Aist. 2006. Incrementally segmenting incoming speech into pragmatic fragments. In *The Third Midwest Computational Linguistics Colloquium (MCLC-2006)*, Urbana, USA.

Michaela Atterer, Timo Baumann, and David Schlangen. 2008. Towards incremental end-of-utterance detection in dialogue systems. In *Proceedings of Coling 2008*, Manchester, UK.

Hermann Helbig and Sven Hartrumpf. 1997. Word class functions for syntactic-semantic analysis. In

Proceedings of the 2nd International Conference on Recent Advances in Natural Language Processing (RANLP'97).

I. Lewin, R. Becket, J. Boye, D. Carter, M. Rayner, and M. Wiren. 1999. Language processing for spoken dialogue systems: is shallow parsing enough? In *Accessing Information in Spoken Audio: Proceedings of ESCA ETRW Workshop*, Cambridge, USA.

George A. Miller, Richard Beckwith, Christiane Fellbaum, Derek Gross, and Katherine Miller. 1993. Five papers on wordnet. Technical report, Princeton University.

David Milward. 2000. Distributing representation for robust interpretation of dialogue utterances. In *Proceedings of ACL 2000*, pages 133–141.

Joakim Nivre. 2004. Incrementality in deterministic dependency parsing. In Frank Keller, Stephen Clark, Matthew Crocker, and Mark Steedman, editors, *Proceedings of the ACL Workshop Incremental Parsing: Bringing Engineering and Cognition Together*, pages 50–57, Barcelona, Spain, July. Association for Computational Linguistics.

M. Rayner, B.A. Hockey, and P. Bouillon. 2006. *Putting Linguistics into Speech Recognition: The Regulus Grammar Compiler*. CSLI Press, Chicago.

Carolyn P. Rose. 2000. A framework for robust semantic interpretation. In *Procs of NACL*.

Yoav Seginer. 2007. Fast unsupervised incremental parsing. In *Proceedings of ACL*, Prague, Czech Republic.

E. Selkirk. 1984. *Phonology and Syntax. The relation between sound and structure*. MIT Press, Cambridge, USA.

Alexander Siebert and David Schlangen. 2008. A simple method for resolution of definite reference in a shared visual context. In *Procs of SIGdial*, Columbus, Ohio.

Alexander Siebert. 2007. Maschinelles Lernen der Bedeutung referenzierender und relationaler Ausdrücke in einem Brettspieldialog. Diploma Thesis, University of Potsdam.

Gabriel Skantze and David Schlangen. 2009. Incremental dialogue processing in a micro-domain. In *Proceedings of EACL 2009*, Athens, Greece, April.

Gabriel Skantze. 2007. *Error Handling in Spoken Dialogue Systems*. Ph.D. thesis, KTH, Stockholm.

Scott C. Stoness, Joel Tetreault, and James Allen. 2004. Incremental parsing with reference interaction. In Frank Keller, Stephen Clark, Matthew Crocker, and Mark Steedman, editors, *Proceedings of the ACL Workshop Incremental Parsing: Bringing Engineering and Cognition Together*, Barcelona, Spain, July.

David R. Traum, Lenhart K. Schubert, Massimo Poesio, Nathaniel G. Martin, Marc Light, Chung Hee Hwang, P. Heeman, George Ferguson, and James Allen. 1996. Knowledge representation in the trains-93 conversation system. *International Journal of Expert Systems*, 9(1):173–223.

Wayne H. Ward. 2008. The phoenix parser user manual. http://cslr.colorado.edu/ whw/phoenix/phoenix_manual.htm.

Klaus Zechner. 1998. Automatic construction of frame representations for spontaneous speech in unrestricted domains. In *Proceedings of COLING-ACL 1998*, Montreal, Canada.

Incrementality, Speaker-Hearer Switching and the Disambiguation Challenge

Ruth Kempson, Eleni Gregoromichelaki
King's College London
{ruth.kempson, eleni.gregor}@kcl.ac.uk

Yo Sato
University of Hertfordshire
y.sato@herts.ac.uk

Abstract

Taking so-called *split utterances* as our point of departure, we argue that a new perspective on the major challenge of disambiguation becomes available, given a framework in which both parsing and generation incrementally involve the same mechanisms for constructing trees reflecting interpretation (*Dynamic Syntax*: (Cann et al., 2005; Kempson et al., 2001)). With all dependencies, syntactic, semantic and pragmatic, defined in terms of incremental progressive tree growth, the phenomenon of speaker/hearer role-switch emerges as an immediate consequence, with the potential for clarification, acknowledgement, correction, all available incrementally at any sub-sentential point in the interpretation process. Accordingly, at all intermediate points where interpretation of an utterance subpart is not fully determined for the hearer in context, uncertainty can be resolved immediately by suitable clarification/correction/repair/extension as an exchange between interlocutors. The result is a major check on the combinatorial explosion of alternative structures and interpretations at each choice point, and the basis for a model of how interpretation in context can be established without either party having to make assumptions about what information they and their interlocutor share in resolving ambiguities.

1 Introduction

A major characteristic of dialogue is effortless switching between the roles of hearer and speaker. Dialogue participants seamlessly shift between parsing and generation bi-directionally across any syntactic dependency, without any indication of there being any problem associated with such shifts (examples from Howes et al. (in prep)):

(1) Conversation from A and B, to C:
A: We're going
B: to Bristol, where Jo lives.

(2) A smelling smoke comes into the kitchen:
A: Have you burnt
B the buns. Very thoroughly.
A: But did you burn
B: Myself? No. Luckily.

(3) A: Are you left or
B: Right-handed.

Furthermore, in no case is there any guarantee that the way the shared utterance evolves is what either party had in mind to say at the outset, indeed obviously not, as otherwise the exchange risks being otiose. This flexibility provides a vehicle for ongoing clarification, acknowledgement, corrections, repairs etc. ((6)-(7) from (Mills, 2007)):

(4) A: I'm seeing Bill.
B: The builder?
A: Yeah, who lives with Monica.

(5) A: I saw Don
B: John?
A: Don, the guy from Bristol.

(6) A: I'm on the second switch
B: Switch?
A: Yeah, the grey thing

(7) A: I'm on the second row third on the left.
B: What?
A: on the left

The fragmental utterances that constitute such incremental, joint contributions have been analysed as falling into discrete structural types according to their function, in all cases resolved to propositional types by combining with appropriate abstractions from context (Fernández, 2006; Purver, 2004). However, any such fragment and their resolution may occur as mid-turn interruptions, well before any emergent propositional structure is completed:

Proceedings of EACL 2009 Workshop on Semantic Representation of Spoken Language - SRSL 2009, pages 74–81,
Athens, Greece, 30 March 2009.

(8) A: They X-rayed me, and took a urine sample, took a blood sample.
Er, the doctor ...

B: Chorlton?

A: Chorlton, mhm, he examined me, erm, he, he said now they were on about a slight [shadow] on my heart. [BNC: KPY 1005-1008]

The advantage of such ongoing, incremental, joint conversational contributions is the effective narrowing down of the search space out of which hearers select (a) interpretations to yield some commonly shared understanding, e.g. choice of referents for NPs, and, (b) restricted structural frames which allow (grammatical) context-dependent fragment resolution, i.e. exact specifications of what contextually available structures resolve elliptical elements. This seems to provide an answer as to why such fragments are so frequent and undemanding elements of dialogue, forming the basis for the observed *coordination* between participants: successive resolution at sub-sentential stages yields a progressively jointly established common ground, that can thereafter be taken as a secure, albeit individual, basis for filtering out interpretations inconsistent with such confirmed knowledge-base (see (Poesio and Rieser, 2008; Ginzburg, forthcmg) etc). All such dialogue phenomena, illustrated in (1)-(8), jointly and incrementally achieved, we address with the general term *split utterances*.

However, such exchanges are hard to model within orthodox grammatical frameworks, given that usually it is the sentence/proposition that is taken as the unit of syntactic/semantic analysis; and they have not been addressed in detail within such frameworks, being set aside as deviant, given that such grammars in principle do not specify a concept of *grammaticality* that relies on a description of the context of occurrence of a certain structure (however, see Poesio and Rieser (2008) for German *completions*). In so far as fragment utterances are now being addressed, the pressure of compatibility with sentence-based grammars is at least partly responsible for analyses of e.g. clarificatory-request fragments as sentential in nature (Ginzburg and Cooper, 2004). But such analyses fail to provide a basis for incrementally resolved clarification requests such as the interruption in (8) where no sentential basis is yet available over which to define the required abstraction of contextually provided content.

In the psycholinguistic literature, on the other hand, there is broad agreement that *incrementality* is a crucial feature of parsing with semantic interpretation taking place as early as possible at the sub-sentential level (see e.g. (Sturt and Crocker, 1996)). Nonetheless, this does not, in and of itself, provide a basis for explaining the ease and frequency of split utterances in dialogue: the interactive coordination between the parsing and production activities, one feeding the other, remains as a challenge.

In NLP modelling, parsing and generation algorithms are generally dissociated from the description of linguistic entities and rules, i.e. the grammar formalisms, which are considered either to be independent of processing ('process-neutral') or to require some additional generation- or parsing-specific mechanisms to be incorporated. However, this point of view creates obstacles for a successful account of data as in (1)-(8). Modelling those would require that, for the current speaker, the initiated generation mechanism has to be displaced mid-production without the propositional generation task having been completed. Then the parsing mechanism, despite being independent of, indeed in some sense the reverse of, the generation component, has to take over mid-sentence as though, in some sense there had been parsing involved up to the point of switchover. Conversely, for the hearer-turned-speaker, it would be necessary to somehow connect their parse with what they are now about to produce in order to compose the meaning of the combined sentence. Moreover, in both directions of switch, as (2) shows, this is not a phenomenon of both interlocutors intending to say the same sentence: as (3) shows, even the function of the utterance (e.g. question/answer) can alter in the switch of roles and such fragments can play two roles (e.g. question/completion) at the same time (e.g. (2)). Hence the grammatical integration of such joint contributions must be flexible enough to allow such switches which means that such fragment resolutions must occur before the computation of intentions at the pragmatic level. So the ability of language users to successfully process such utterances, even at sub-sentential levels, means that modelling their grammar requires fine-grained grammaticality definitions able to characterise and integrate sub-sentential fragments in turns jointly constructed by speaker and hearer.

This can be achieved straightforwardly if features like incrementality and context-dependent processing are built into the grammar architecture itself. The modelling of split utterances then becomes straightforward as each successive processing step exploits solely the grammatical apparatus to succeed or fail. Such a view notably does not invoke high-level decisions about speaker/hearer intentions as part of the mechanism itself. That this is the right view to take is enhanced by the fact that as all of (1)-(8) show, neither party in such role-exchanges can definitively know in advance what will emerge as the eventual joint proposition. If, to the contrary, generation decisions are modelled as involving intentions for whole utterances, there will be no the basis for modelling how such incomplete strings can be integrated in suitable contexts, with joint propositional structures emerging before such *joint intentions* have been established.

An additional puzzle, equally related to both the challenges of disambiguation and the status of modelling speaker's intentions as part of the mechanism whereby utterance interpretation takes place, is the common occurrence of hearers NOT being constrained by any check on consistency with speaker intentions in determining a putative interpretation, failing to make use of well established shared knowledge:

(9) A: I'm going to cook salmon, as John's coming.
B: What? John's a vegetarian.
A: Not my brother. John Smith.

(10) A: Why don't you have cheese and noodles?
B: Beef? You KNOW I'm a vegetarian

Such examples are problematic for any account that proposes that interpretation mechanisms for utterance understanding solely depend on selection of interpretations which either the speaker could have intended (Sperber and Wilson, 1986; Carston, 2002), or ones which are compatible with checking consistency with the common ground/plans established between speaker and hearer (Poesio and Rieser, 2008; Ginzburg, forthcmg), mutual knowledge, etc. (Clark, 1996; Brennan and Clark, 1996). To the contrary, the data in (9)-(10) tend to show that the full range of interpretations computable by the grammar has in principle to be available at all choice points for construal, without any filter based on plausibility measures, thus leaving the disambiguation challenge still unresolved.

In this paper we show how with speaker and hearer in principle using the same mechanisms for construal, equally incrementally applied, such disambiguation issues can be resolved in a timely manner which in turn reduces the multiplication of structural/interpretive options. As we shall see, what connects our diverse examples, and indeed underpins the smooth shift in the joint endeavour of conversation, lies in *incremental*, context-dependent processing and *bidirectionality*, essential ingredients of the *Dynamic Syntax* (Cann et al., 2005) dialogue model.

2 Incrementality in Dynamic Syntax

Dynamic Syntax (*DS*) is a procedure-oriented framework, involving incremental processing, i.e. strictly sequential, word-by-word interpretation of linguistic strings. The notion of incrementality in DS is closely related to another of its features, the *goal-directedness* of BOTH parsing and generation. At each stage of processing, *structural predictions* are triggered that could fulfill the goals compatible with the input, in an underspecified manner. For example, when a proper name like *Bob* is encountered sentence-initially in English, a semantic predicate node is predicted to follow ($?Ty(e \rightarrow t)$), amongst other possibilities.

By way of introducing the reader to the DS devices, let us look at some formal details with an example, *Bob saw Mary*. The 'complete' semantic representation tree resulting after the complete processing of this sentence is shown in Figure 2 below. A DS tree is formally encoded with the tree logic *LOFT* (Blackburn and Meyer-Viol (1994)), we omit these details here) and is generally binary configurational, with annotations at every node. Important annotations here, see the (simplified) tree below, are those which represent semantic formulae along with their type information (e.g. '$Ty(x)$') based on a combination of the epsilon and lambda calculi[1].

Such complete trees are constructed, starting from a radically underspecified annotation, the *axiom*, the leftmost minimal tree in Figure 2, and going through *monotonic updates* of partial, or *structurally underspecified*, trees. The outline of this process is illustrated schematically in Figure 2. Crucial for expressing the goal-directedness are *requirements*, i.e. unrealised but expected

[1]These are the adopted semantic representation languages in DS but the computational formalism is compatible with other semantic-representation formats

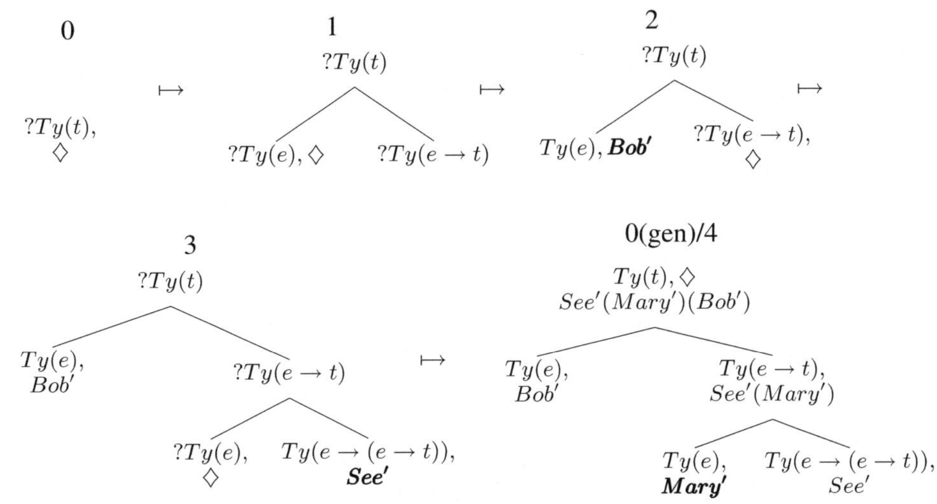

Figure 2: Monotonic tree growth in DS

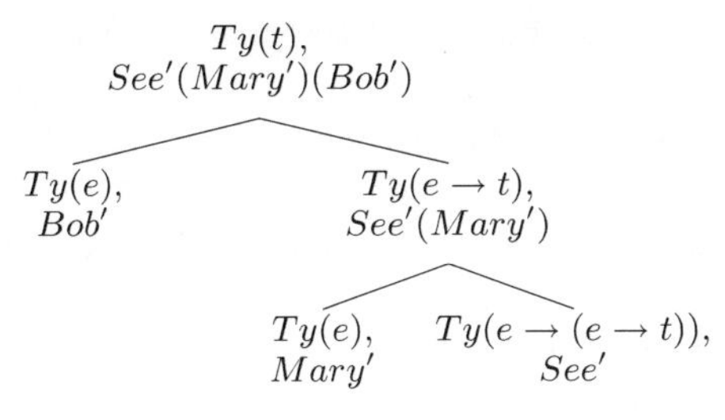

Figure 1: A DS complete tree

node/tree specifications, indicated by '?' in front of annotations. The axiom says that a proposition (of type *t*, $Ty(t)$) is expected to be constructed. Furthermore, the *pointer*, notated with '◇' indicates the 'current' node in processing, namely the one to be processed next, and governs word order.

Updates are carried out by means of applying *actions*, which are divided into two types. *Computational actions* govern general tree-constructional processes, such as moving the pointer, introducing and updating nodes, as well as compiling interpretation for all non-terminal nodes in the tree. In our example, the update of (1) to (2) is executed via computational actions specific to English, expanding the axiom to the subject and predicate nodes, requiring the former to be processed next by the position of the ◇. Construction of only weakly specified tree relations (*unfixed nodes*) can also be induced, characterised only as dominance by some current node, with subsequent update required. Individual lexical items also provide procedures for building structure in the form of *lexical actions*, inducing both nodes and annotations. For example, in the update from (2) to (3), the set of lexical actions for the word *see* is applied, yielding the predicate subtree and its annotations. Thus *partial trees* grow incrementally, driven by procedures associated with particular words as they are encountered.

Requirements embody structural predictions as mentioned earlier. Thus unlike the conventional bottom-up parsing,[2] the DS model takes the parser/generator to entertain some predicted *goal(s)* to be reached eventually at any stage of processing, and this is precisely what makes the formalism incremental. This is the characterisation of incrementality adopted by some psycholinguists under the appellation of *connectedness* (Sturt and Crocker, 1996; Costa et al., 2002): an encountered word always gets 'connected' to a larger, predicted, tree.

Individual DS trees consist of predicates and their arguments. Complex structures are obtained via a general tree-adjunction operation licensing the construction of so-called *LINKed* trees, pairs of trees where sharing of information occurs. In its simplest form this mechanism is the same one which provides the potential for compiling in-

[2] The examples in (1)-(8) also suggest the implausibility of purely bottom-up or head-driven parsing being adopted directly, because such strategies involve waiting until all the daughters are gathered before moving on to their projection. In fact, the parsing strategy adopted by DS is somewhat similar to mixed parsing strategies like the left-corner or Earley algorithm to a degree. These parsing strategic issues are more fully discussed in Sato (forthcmg).

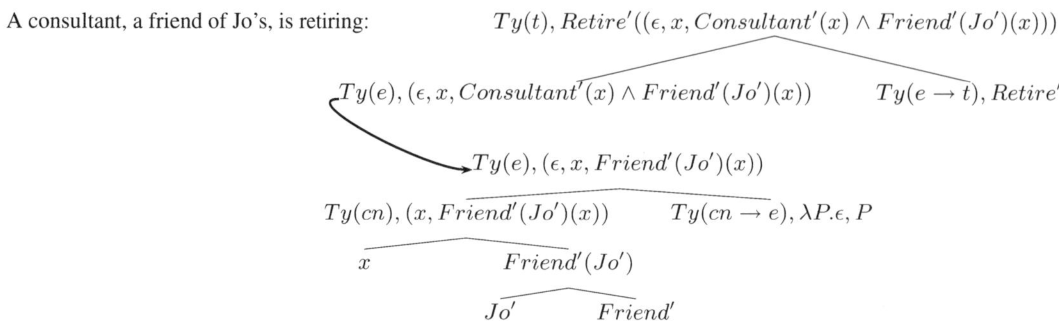

Figure 3: Apposition in DS

terpretation for *apposition* constructions as can be seen in Figure (3)[3]. The assumption in the construction of such LINKed structures is that at any arbitrary stage of development, some type-complete subtree may constitute the context for the subsequent parsing of the following string as an adjunct structure candidate for incorporation into the primary tree, hence the obligatory sharing of information in the resulting semantic representation.

More generally, *context* in DS is defined as the storage of *parse states*, i.e., the storing of partial tree, word sequence parsed to date, plus the actions used in building up the partial tree. Formally, a parse state P is defined as a set of triples $\langle T, W, A\rangle$, where: T is a (possibly partial) tree; W is the associated sequence of words; A is the associated sequence of lexical and computational actions. At any point in the parsing process, the context $\mathcal{C}$ for a particular partial tree T in the set P can be taken to consist of: a set of triples $P' = \{\ldots, \langle T_i, W_i, A_i\rangle, \ldots\}$ resulting from the previous sentence(s); and the triple $\langle T, W, A\rangle$ itself, the subtree currently being processed. Anaphora and ellipsis construal generally involve re-use of formulae, structures, and actions from the set $\mathcal{C}$. *Grammaticality* of a string of words is then defined relative to its context $\mathcal{C}$, a string being well-formed iff there is a mapping from string onto completed tree with no outstanding requirements given the monotonic processing of that string relative to context. All fragments illustrated above are processed by means of either extending the current tree, or constructing LINKed structures and transfer of information among them so that one tree provides the context for another, and are licensed as wellformed relative to that context. In particular, fragments like *the doctor* in (8) are licensed by the grammar because they occur at a stage in processing at which the context contains an appropriate structure within which they can be integrated. The definite NP is taken as an anaphoric device, relying on a substitution process from the context of the partial tree to which the node it decorates is LINKed to achieve the appropriate construal and tree-update:

(11) The"parse" tree licensing production of *the doctor*: LINK adjunction

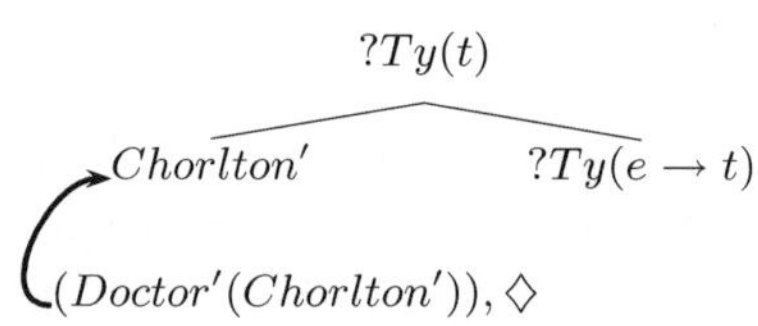

3 Bidirectionality in DS

Crucially, for our current concern, this architecture allows a dialogue model in which generation and parsing function in parallel, following exactly the same procedure in the same order. See Fig (2) for a (simplified) display of the transitions manipulated by a parse of *Bob saw Mary*, as each word is processed and integrated to reach the complete tree. Generation of this utterance from a complete tree follows precisely the same actions and trees from left to right, although the complete tree is available from the start (this is why the complete tree is marked '0' for generation): in this case the eventual message is known by the speaker, though of course not by the hearer. What generation involves in addition to the parse steps is reference

[3] *Epsilon terms*, like $\epsilon, x, Consultant'(x)$, stand for witnesses of existentially quantified formulae in the epsilon calculus and represent the semantic content of indefinites in DS. Defined relative to the equivalence $\psi(\epsilon, x, \psi(x)) = \exists x \psi(x)$, their defining property is their reflection of their containing environment, and accordingly they are particularly well-suited to expressing the growth of terms secured by such appositional devices.

to this complete tree to check whether each putative step is consistent with it in order not to be deviated from the legitimate course of action, that is, a *subsumption* check. The trees (1-3) are licensed because each of these subsumes (4). Each time then the generator applies a lexical action, it is licensed to produce the word that carries that action under successful subsumption check: at Step (3), for example, the generator processes the lexical action which results in the annotation 'See'', and upon success and subsumption of (4) license to generate the word *see* at that point ensues.

For split utterances, two more assumptions are pertinent. On the one hand, speakers may have initially only a partial structure to convey: this is unproblematic, as all that is required by the formalism is monotonicity of tree growth, the check being one of *subsumption* which can be carried out on partial trees as well. On the other hand, the utterance plan may change, even within a single speaker. Extensions and clarifications in DS can be straightforwardly generated by appending a LINKed structure projecting the added material to be conveyed (preserving the monotonicity constraint)[4].

(12) I'm going home, with my brother, maybe with his wife.

Such a model under which the speaker and hearer essentially follow the same sets of actions, updating incrementally their semantic representations, allows the hearer to 'mirror' the same series of partial trees, albeit not knowing in advance what the content of the unspecified nodes will be.

4 Parser/generator implementation

The process-integral nature of DS emphasised thus far lends itself to the straightforward implementation of a parsing/generating system, since the 'actions' defined in the grammar directly provide a major part of its implementation. By now it should also be clear that the DS formalism is fully bi-directional, not only in the sense that the same grammar can be used for generation and parsing, but also because the two sets of activities, conventionally treated as 'reverse' processes, are modelled to run in parallel. Therefore, not only can the same sets of actions be used for both processes, but also a large part of the parsing and generation algorithms can be shared.

This design architecture and a prototype implementation are outlined in (Purver and Otsuka, 2003), and the effort is under way to scale up the DS parsing/generating system incorporating the results in (Gargett et al., 2008; Gregoromichelaki et al., to appear).[5] The parser starts from the axiom (step 0 in Fig.2), which 'predicts' a proposition to be built, and follows the applicable actions, lexical or general, to develop a complete tree. Now, as has been described in this paper, the generator follows exactly the same steps: the axiom is developed through successive updates into a complete tree. The only material difference from – or rather in addition to– parsing is the complete tree (Step 0(gen)/4), given from the very start of the generation task, which is then referred to at each tree update for *subsumption* check. The main point is that despite the obvious difference in their purposes –outputting a string from a meaning versus outputting a meaning from a string– parsing and generation indeed share the *direction* of processing in DS. Moreover, as no intervening level of syntactic structure over the string is ever computed, the parsing/generation tasks are more efficiently incremental in that semantic interpretation is directly imposed at each stage of lexical integration, irrespective of whether some given partially developed constituent is complete.

To clarify, see the pseudocode in the Prolog format below, which is a close analogue of the implemented function that both does parsing and generation of a word (context manipulation is ignored here for reasons of space). The plus and minus signs attached to a variable indicate it must/needn't be instantiated, respectively. In effect, the former corresponds to the input, the latter to the output.

(13)
```
parse_gen_word(
    +OldMeaning,±Word,±NewMeaning):-
        apply_lexical_actions(+OldMeaning, ±Word,
        +LexActions, −IntermediateMeaning ),
        apply_computational_actions(
        +IntermediateMeaning, +CompActions,
        ±NewMeaning )
```

OldMeaning is an obligatory input item, which corresponds to the semantic structure constructed so far (which might be just structural tree information initially before any lexical

[4]Revisions however will involve shifting to a previous partial tree as the newly selected context: *I'm going home, to my brother, sorry my mother.*

[5]The preliminary results are described in (Sato, forthcmg).

input has been processed thus advocating a strong predictive element even compared to (Sturt and Crocker, 1996). Now notice that the other two variables —corresponding to the word and the new (post-word) meaning— may function either as the input or output. More precisely, this is intended to be a shorthand for either (+OldMeaning,+Word,−NewMeaning) i.e. Word as input and NewMeaning as output, or (+OldMeaning,−Word,+NewMeaning), i.e. NewMeaning as input and Word as output, to repeat, the former corresponding to parsing and the latter to generation.

In either case, the same set of two sub-procedures, the two kinds of actions described in (13), are applied sequentially to process the input to produce the output. These procedures correspond to an incremental 'update' from one partial tree to another, through a word. The whole function is then recursively applied to exhaust the words in the string, from left to right, either in parsing or generation. Thus there is no difference between the two in the order of procedures to be applied, or words to be processed. Thus it is a mere switch of input/output that shifts between parsing and generation.[6]

4.1 Split utterances in Dynamic Syntax

Split utterances follow as an immediate consequence of these assumptions. For the dialogues in (1)-(8), therefore, while A reaches a partial tree of what she has uttered through successive updates as described above, B as the hearer, will follow the same updates to reach the same representation of what he has heard. This provides him with the ability at any stage to become the speaker, interrupting to continue A's utterance, repair, ask for clarification, reformulate, or provide a correction, as and when necessary[7]. According to our model of dialogue, repeating or extending a constituent of A's utterance by B is licensed only if B, the hearer turned now speaker, entertains a message to be conveyed that matches or extends the parse tree of what he has heard in a monotonic fashion. In DS, this message is a semantic representation in tree format and its presence allows B to only utter the relevant subpart of A's intended utterance. Indeed, this update is what B is seeking to clarify, extend or acknowledge. In DS, B can reuse the already constructed (partial) parse tree in his context, rather than having to rebuild an entire propositional tree or subtree.

The fact that the parsing formalism integrates a strong element of *predictivity*, i.e. the parser is always one step ahead from the lexical input, allows a straightforward switch from parsing to generation thus resulting in an explanation of the facility with which split utterances occur (even without explicit reasoning processes). Moreover, on the one hand, because of *incrementality*, the issue of interpretation-selection can be faced at any point in the process, with corrections/acknowledgements etc. able to be provided at any point; this results in the potential exponential explosion of interpretations being kept firmly in check. And, structurally, such fragments can be integrated in the current partial tree representation only (given the position of the pointer) so there is no structural ambiguity multiplication. On the other hand, for any one of these intermediate check points, *bidirectionality* entails that consistency checking remains internal to the individual interlocutors' system, the fact of their mirroring each other resulting at their being at the same point of tree growth. This is sufficient to ensure that any inconsistency with their own parse recognised by one party as grounds for correction/repair can be processed AS a correction/repair by the other party without requiring any additional metarepresentation of their interlocutors' information state (at least for these purposes). This allows the possibility of building up apparently complex assumptions of shared content, without any necessity of constructing hypotheses of what is entertained by the other, since all context-based selections are based on the context of the interlocutor themselves. This, in its turn, opens up the possibility of hearers constructing interpretations based on selections made that transparently violate what is knowledge shared by both parties, for no presumption of common ground is essential as input to the interpretation process (see, e.g. (9)-(10)).

[6]Thus the parsing procedure is dictated by the grammar to a large extent, but importantly, not completely. More specifically, the grammar formalism specifies the state paths themselves, but not *how* the paths should be searched. The DS actions are defined in conditional terms, i.e. what to do as and when a certain condition holds. If a number of actions can be applied at some point during a parse, i.e. locally ambiguity is encountered, then it is up to a particular implementation of the parser to decide which should be traversed first. The current implementation includes suggestions of search strategies.

[7]The account extends the implementation reported in (Purver et al., 2006)

5 Conclusion

It is notable that, from this perspective, no presumption of common ground or hypothesis as to what the speaker could have intended is necessary to determine how the hearer selects interpretation. All that is required is a concept of system-internal consistency checking, the potential for clarification in cases of uncertainty, and reliance at such points on disambiguation/correction/repair by the other party. The advantage of such a proposal, we suggest, is the provision of a fully mechanistic account for disambiguation (cf. (Pickering and Garrod, 2004)). The consequence of such an analysis is that language use is essentially interactive (see also (Ginzburg, forthcmg; Clark, 1996)): the only constraint as to whether some hypothesised interpretation assigned by either party is confirmed turns on whether it is acknowledged or corrected (see also (Healey, 2008)).

Acknowledgements

This work was supported by grants ESRC RES-062-23-0962, the EU ITALK project (FP7-214668) and Leverhulme F07-04OU. We are grateful for comments to: Robin Cooper, Alex Davies, Arash Eshghi, Jonathan Ginzburg, Pat Healey, Greg James Mills. Normal disclaimers apply.

References

Patrick Blackburn and Wilfried Meyer-Viol. 1994. Linguistics, logic and finite trees. *Bulletin of the IGPL*, 2:3–31.

Susan E. Brennan and Herbert H. Clark. 1996. Conceptual pacts and lexical choice in conversation. *Journal of Experimental Psychology: Learning, Memory and Cognition*, 22:482–1493.

Ronnie Cann, Ruth Kempson, and Lutz Marten. 2005. *The Dynamics of Language*. Elsevier, Oxford.

Robyn Carston. 2002. *Thoughts and Utterances: The Pragmatics of Explicit Communication*. Blackwell.

Herbert H. Clark. 1996. *Using Language*. Cambridge University Press.

Fabrizio Costa, Paolo Frasconi, Vincenzo Lombardo, Patrick Sturt, and Giovanni Soda. 2002. Enhancing first-pass attachment prediction. In *ECAI 2002: 508-512*.

Raquel Fernández. 2006. *Non-Sentential Utterances in Dialogue: Classification, Resolution and Use*. Ph.D. thesis, King's College London, University of London.

Andrew Gargett, Eleni Gregoromichelaki, Chris Howes, and Yo Sato. 2008. Dialogue-grammar correspondence in dynamic syntax. In *Proceedings of the 12th SEMDIAL (LONDIAL)*.

Jonathan Ginzburg and Robin Cooper. 2004. Clarification, ellipsis, and the nature of contextual updates in dialogue. *Linguistics and Philosophy*, 27(3):297–365.

Jonathan Ginzburg. forthcmg. *Semantics for Conversation*. CSLI.

Eleni Gregoromichelaki, Yo Sato, Ruth Kempson, Andrew Gargett, and Christine Howes. to appear. Dialogue modelling and the remit of core grammar. In *Proceedings of IWCS 2009*.

Patrick Healey. 2008. Interactive misalignment: The role of repair in the development of group sublanguages. In R. Cooper and R. Kempson, editors, *Language in Flux*. College Publications.

Christine Howes, Patrick G. T. Healey, and Gregory Mills. in prep. a: An experimental investigation into... b: ... split utterances.

Ruth Kempson, Wilfried Meyer-Viol, and Dov Gabbay. 2001. *Dynamic Syntax: The Flow of Language Understanding*. Blackwell.

Gregory J. Mills. 2007. *Semantic co-ordination in dialogue: the role of direct interaction*. Ph.D. thesis, Queen Mary University of London.

Martin Pickering and Simon Garrod. 2004. Toward a mechanistic psychology of dialogue. *Behavioral and Brain Sciences*.

Massimo Poesio and Hannes Rieser. 2008. Completions, coordination, and alignment in dialogue. Ms.

Matthew Purver and Masayuki Otsuka. 2003. Incremental generation by incremental parsing: Tactical generation in Dynamic Syntax. In *Proceedings of the 9th European Workshop in Natural Language Generation (ENLG)*, pages 79–86.

Matthew Purver, Ronnie Cann, and Ruth Kempson. 2006. Grammars as parsers: Meeting the dialogue challenge. *Research on Language and Computation*, 4(2-3):289–326.

Matthew Purver. 2004. *The Theory and Use of Clarification Requests in Dialogue*. Ph.D. thesis, University of London, forthcoming.

Yo Sato. forthcmg. Local ambiguity, search strategies and parsing in dynamic syntax. In Eleni Gregoromichelaki and Ruth Kempson, editors, *Dynamic Syntax: Collected Papers*. CSLI.

Dan Sperber and Deirdre Wilson. 1986. *Relevance: Communication and Cognition*. Blackwell.

Patrick Sturt and Matthew Crocker. 1996. Monotonic syntactic processing: a cross-linguistic study of attachment and reanalysis. *Language and Cognitive Processes*, 11:448–494.

Author Index